TOMATOES
A Gardener's Guide

TOMATOES

A Gardener's Guide

Simon Hart

THE CROWOOD PRESS

First published in 2010 by
The Crowood Press Ltd
Ramsbury, Marlborough
Wiltshire SN8 2HR

www.crowood.com

British Library Cataloguing-in-Publication Data
A catalogue record for this book is available from the British Library.

ISBN 978 1 84797 199 9

Photographic Acknowledgements
All photographs by the author, except where otherwise credited: frontispiece and pages 6, 13, 42, 106 and 121 © Rhoda Nottridge; pages 11 and 16 © Tony Bundock; page 25 © Sue Bunwell and Andrew Davis; pages 26, 114, 115 and 116 © Delfland Nurseries. Photographs on pages 7, 8, 10, 21, 22, 37–39, 44, 56, 57, 62, 64, 76, 85, 88, 107 and 117–119 were taken in the greenhouses of Writtle College, Essex.

Illustrations by Caroline Pratt

Typeset by Jean Cussons Typesetting, Diss, Norfolk

Printed and bound in Singapore by Craft Print International

CONTENTS

1 TOMATO HISTORY

The original wild tomatoes come from South America, and can still be found in Peru, Bolivia, Ecuador, Chile and Colombia. Rather oddly there is no word for the plant in early South American Indian languages, and certainly no record of its cultivation, so it seems unlikely that any of the early local inhabitants found a use for it. Of the thirteen wild species considered as 'tomatoes', no single one of these is recognized as being the direct ancestor of the modern cultivated tomato, though genetically the closest relative is the tiny fruited *Lycopersicon pimpinellifolium*, or redcurrant tomato.

The first cultivation of the tomato appears to have been by the Aztecs in what is now Mexico, some 2,000 miles distant from its native region. When the Spanish conquistadors arrived they found an advanced agricultural system, and yellow-fruited tomatoes being grown. How the Aztecs got their hands on the original plants from 2,000 miles away is something of a mystery, though a believable theory is that over time, seeds of the plants would have had found their way into the area courtesy of migrating birds. Tomato seeds are well known for their ability to pass through the digestive tract, as the stories of bumper crops of tomato plants found at sewage treatment works will support.

The tomato made its way into Europe, and also into Spanish colonies in North America and the Caribbean, in the very early 1500s, although some attribute its introduction into Europe to Columbus as early as 1498. As the first tomatoes to appear in Europe were the yellow-fruited form, they gained the name 'pomo d'oro' or 'golden apple', which remains the same in Italian to this day. The tomato gets a mention in several of the early herbals from the mid-1500s and 1600s. Writing in 1550, Pier Andrea Mattioli used the Italian name 'pomodoro' – but he also mentioned that there was a red form of the fruit.

Initially no one seemed particularly impressed by the fruit; though edible it was identified as a close cousin of the deadly nightshade, so became regarded as slightly suspicious, if not quite as dangerous as its relative.

The date of the introduction of the tomato to England is usually given as 1596, but was almost certainly earlier as the first description of the fruit in the English language came courtesy of John Gerard in his *Herball* of 1597. Gerard was also fairly unimpressed, writing: 'In Spaine and those hot regions they used to eate the apples prepared and boil'd with pepper, salt and oyle, but they yeeld very little nourishment to the bodie.'

OPPOSITE: **Nutritious and delicious, the tomato is a favourite crop for the gardener.**

RIGHT: **'Black Russian', an interesting old heritage cultivar.**

ABOVE: Flowers of *Lycopersicon penellii*.

LEFT: *Lycopersicon penellii* – a 'wild' tomato.

By the end of the sixteenth century the red-fruited form had become more commonplace, and in England had picked up the common name 'love apple'; the reason for this is lost in history, possible theories ranging from the associations with the red colour of the fruit, to a misinterpretation of the name 'pomodoro' as 'pomi de moro' ('apple of the Moors', or 'Spanish') and then to the French 'pomme d'amour'. Whatever the origin, a reputation for aphrodisiac qualities stuck by association, and consequently the English were a bit nervous about eating the fruit, growing the plant principally as a botanical curiosity and for its ornamental value. (Interestingly the potato once commanded high prices in parts of Europe due to its reputation as an aphrodisiac, though this is more likely to have been a cunning bit of marketing than something connected with the *Solanaceae* in general.)

There does not appear to be a particular point at which the tomato made the transition from ornamental to edible; it is most likely that it caught on gradually. Hannah Glasse's cookbook *The Art of Cookery* of 1758 lists a tomato recipe.

It took until 1822 for the first specific instructions for the cultivation of the tomato to appear, by which time they were already being produced for sale in the south of England, though their popularity was not great. In William Cobbett's *The English Gardener* of 1829 the whole subject of the production of 'tomatum' is disposed of in half a page, whereas the other salad staple, the cucumber, is indulged for a full nine pages. Cobbett appears fairly disinterested in the tomato, writing: 'The fruit is used for various purposes, and sold at a pretty high price.'

AGREEING ON A NAME

In the novel *Lark Rise to Candleford* (set in the late 1800s) Flora Thompson describes the first appearance of red and yellow tomatoes on the local peddler's cart, saying that they had 'Not long been introduced into the country, and were slowly making their way into favour'. Struck by the colours, the girl Laura asks what they are, and is told: 'Love apples, me dear, love apples, they be; though some hignorant folk be calling them tommy-toes.' The name 'tomato' appears to have come by a rather roundabout route from the Aztec *Xitomatl* or *Tomatl*, via the seventeenth-century Spanish *tomate*, by way of *tomata* in England and America in the 1800s (Dickens uses the word 'tomata' in *The Pickwick Papers*) to the 'tomato' of today.

Latin Origins: the Edible Wolf Peach

The Latin name given to the tomato is *Lycopersicon esculentum*, which translates as the 'edible wolf peach'. The origin of the name *Lycopersicon* is attributed to the Greek naturalist Galen (129–207AD), but whatever plant Galen was describing it certainly wasn't a tomato, as they didn't appear in the Mediterranean area for another 1,400 years. How the tomato took the name *Lycopersicon* appears to stem from its similarity (particularly in the appearance of the fruit) to another famous member of the Solanaceae family, the belladonna or deadly nightshade. In Germany it was believed that witches used belladonna to conjure werewolves, so Germans considered the name wolf peach quite appropriate.

Linnaeus (1753) classified the tomato as *Solanum lycopersicon*, but Tournefort (1694) had already considered the tomato to be a distinct and separate genus, *Lycopersicon*. Consequently the name *Solanum lycopersicum* is still occasionally

BELOW RIGHT: **Ripe deadly nightshade berries.**

BELOW: **Young deadly nightshade plant** *Atropa belladonna.*

found, but *Lycopersicon esculentum* is the accepted botanical name. The actual taxonomy or botanical classification of tomato is still far from clear, particularly concerning the 'wild' types of tomato. The classification developed by C. H. Muller in his 'A revision of the genus *Lycopersicon*' of 1940 is still commonly used. Muller divides the genus into two sub-genera *Eulycopersicon* and *Eriopersicon*, putting *L. esculentum* into the first sub-genus, as shown below:

Genus: *Lycopersicon*
Sub-genus: *Eulycopersicon*

Lycopersicon esculentum
Lycopersicon esculentum Pyriforme – pear-shaped tomato
Lycopersicon esculentum Cerasiforme – cherry tomato
Lycopersicon pimpinellifolium – redcurrant tomato

Whatever the taxonomists eventually end up agreeing on, it is very convenient that all the 'wild' types of tomato are capable of being cross-bred with the cultivated types (though sometimes this is difficult to achieve), representing a great genetic base for continued crop improvement.

FROM HUMBLE BEGINNINGS TO THE TOMATO OF TODAY

The slow acceptance of the fruit in England – even after the reputation for being a slightly poisonous aphrodisiac had worn off – can be put

The fruit of *lycopersicon penellii* – hairy fruit is typical of the Eriopersicon types, or wild tomatoes.

down to a number of reasons, principally availability. Obviously production was seasonal: in the open ground or walled garden the fruit would only be available in quantity for three months of the year, and production in glasshouses did not start on a commercial scale until the very late 1800s. The first records of tomato crops from the emerging glasshouse industry in the Lea valley (just north of London) date from 1887.

Initially tomatoes would have been more available to city dwellers, as market gardens with greenhouses developed on the fringes of large urban conurbations. The expansion of the railways, increased supplies from the Channel Islands, and the developing greenhouse industry on the south coast of England steadily widened availability. In America, where the tomato had become very popular from the mid-1800s, the growers had a lucky break: in 1893, flying in the face of botanical facts, the US supreme court classed the tomato as a vegetable rather than a fruit, and as all imported vegetables were taxed at the time (whereas fruits were not), supplies from Cuba and Mexico dried up, leaving the way clear for domestic growers to fill the supply gap.

The emerging greenhouse industry took to the tomato as a useful summer crop, grown in rotation with leafy salads and cut flowers, but under the government's push for food production

during World War II it really came of age as a greenhouse crop producing a fruit valuable in the diet for a nation short of its usual sources of vitamins from imported fruits. The gardening public were obviously aware of the value of the tomato: the Ministry of Agriculture's *Allotments and Garden Guide* for June 1945 states that according to their information, the tomato is 'Crop no.1 with war-time gardeners and allotment holders'. Today, with gardens getting smaller, the versatility of the tomato to a range of different cultivation methods is even more apparent. It is reported that 90 per cent of gardeners in the USA cultivate tomatoes.

The annual world production of the tomato is in the region of 110 million metric tonnes from 4.4 million hectares of land, with China being the biggest single producer, followed by the USA.

There is, of course, a world of difference between the production of processing tomatoes, grown as an agricultural crop on a field scale for mechanical harvest, and the production of fresh or salad tomatoes, which are mainly produced as a greenhouse crop. Rather strangely it is countries in northern Europe, a region not climatically ideal for tomato production, that produce the highest yields per hectare by using heated greenhouses, with the Dutch being the leaders in this type of production.

THE TOMATO: FOOD, SUPER FOOD OR MEDICINE?

Considering that many of its cousins in the Solanaceae yield a whole raft of medicinal substances, to date not much use has been made of the tomato in medicine – the juice of the tomato leaf and stem was first used in the sixteenth century to treat skin diseases, but it was not until the 1940s that it was discovered that a substance in the leaves, named tomatine, did halt the growth of fungal disorders such as athlete's foot, and soaps containing leaf and stem extract were marketed for the very purpose. Tomato soaps are still available today, but containing fruit extract and citing the vitamin and anti-oxidant content as being good for the complexion.

Modern large-scale greenhouse tomato production.

The native black nightshade *Solanum nigrum* – a common enough summer weed in the UK and mildly poisonous, though the related African *Solanum scabrum* is edible, and the leaves are used like spinach.

Enter Lycopene

In the USA, patent medicines containing tomato were peddled by the 'snake oil' salesmen of the old West as general cure-alls. Few of these made any commercial impression, but 'Dr Milne's Compound Extract of Tomato', which today would be recognized as tomato ketchup, was probably closer to something with actual medicinal value than the charlatans of the time realized, on account of its lycopene content. Lycopene is a red carotenoid pigment that occurs in a number of fruits, and was first identified in the tomato in 1875. In more recent times it has been recognized as a strong antioxidant and possible anticarcinogen. Lycopene is more available in cooked tomatoes and tomato products (pastes, ketchups) than in the fresh fruit, and as it is fat soluble, tomato products or dishes that include oil also help its absorption.

Gathering a belladonna crop on a UK Materia Medica farm in the 1920s.

CLOSE FAMILY – OTHER *SOLANACEAE* OF INTEREST

A strangely diverse family providing everything from valuable food crops to deadly poisons, twenty-five species of *Solanum* provide staple crops in various parts of the world, though of these only four are grown on a commercial scale in the UK and US: tomato, potato, aubergine or eggplant, and capsicum or pepper. The potato *Solanum tuberosum* provides more calories per unit area of ground than any other food crop, and is the world's most widely consumed vegetable.

The well known poisonous arm of the family, which includes deadly nightshade and henbane, gives us a whole collection of useful drugs used in everything from heart surgery to remedies for seasickness. Both plants were once commercially grown in the south and east of England. The other famous *Solanum*, tobacco, remains the most important world non-food crop in economic terms.

Many other *Solanaceae* have yet to realize their full potential, but are currently creating interest as possible new crops; for example, some leafy species of nightshade native to Africa (close relatives of the UK's black nightshade *Solanum nigrum*), far from being poisonous, are regularly eaten, and are particularly high in vitamins and minerals.

2 THE TOMATO PLANT: PHYSIOLOGY AND VARIETIES

Tomatoes are short-lived perennial plants, which for practical purposes are treated as annuals. In the UK they are classed as tender plants, as they cannot tolerate frosts.

TOMATO PLANT TYPES

The cultivated tomato of today exists in two basic plant forms: the indeterminate and the determinate.

The Indeterminate Type

In the UK the most familiar type is the indeterminate – sometimes known as cordon – as this is the main type grown both commercially as a greenhouse crop and in the back garden. The plant produces a single stem, which appears to have a single growing point from which all extension growth comes. Indeterminate tomatoes usually produce seven or eight leaves before the first flower truss forms, thereafter producing a truss after every two leaves. The number of flowers and therefore fruit that each truss produces is cultivar dependent, but sometimes the first truss on early planted tomatoes is branched (so giving potentially more fruit), whereas later ones are not.

The plant also produces lateral growth or side shoots from axillary buds, so left to its own devices soon becomes an impressive spreading vine. For practical purposes the sideshoots are removed on a regular basis restricting the plant to a single stem, which is then trained up a string or stake. At one time this type of training system picked up the name 'cordon' as it resembles the way single-stemmed cordon apple trees are trained. Some seed merchants describe indeterminate tomato cultivars as cordon types.

'Gardener's delight', an old favourite.

OPPOSITE: The indeterminate, or cordon, tomato is the most commonly-grown type grown in both the greenhouse and the garden.

TRAINING INDETERMINATE TOMATOES

There is no actual need to follow commercial practice and restrict the plant to a single stem when growing indeterminate types, though in a greenhouse it does make sense for ease of management. When grown outdoors indeterminate tomatoes can be grown as multi-stemmed plants by allowing the development of sideshoots, or even used as a feature to cover trellises and similar structures in the way that Victorian gardeners would have used them.

lateral shoots, which also stop growing when flower trusses form. This gives a short plant of bushy appearance, with the final height depending on the cultivar. As the flower trusses develop more or less simultaneously, this means that most of the fruit on the plant ripens over a relatively short period. This trait makes determinate tomatoes very useful in northern latitudes with short growing seasons, and has been further developed in cultivars grown for processing, allowing a one-off destructive harvest in which the plants are pulled up and the fruit combed off mechanically. When grown outdoors under UK conditions, determinate types give the earliest fruit from a spring planting.

When grown in this fashion as a commercial greenhouse crop, the stem can reach 12–14m (40–45ft) in length over a season.

The Determinate or Bush Type

In the UK, the determinate type is perhaps less familiar to gardeners. The plant grows initially as a single stem that produces a flower truss followed by one to two more leaves, then extension growth stops. Further vegetative growth then comes from

Type Variations

There are also cultivars listed as semi-determinate types: these grow initially like an indeterminate, producing a single stem with several flower trusses, but eventually the stem forms a final flower truss and stops extension growth. It then behaves like a bush tomato, with further vegetative growth coming from the sideshoots. Whereas it is often possible to get away with not providing plant supports for indeterminate types, the vigour and tall growth of the semi-determinates will definitely make support necessary.

ABOVE: 'Balconi Yellow', a novelty type small enough to be grown as a windowsill pot.

LEFT: The bush or determinate cultivar 'Sub-Arctic Plenty'.

Bi-locular fruit.

Tri-locular fruit.

Dwarf and miniature novelty types are indeterminate, with very short internodes and a strong stem that makes them essentially self-supporting.

TOMATO FRUIT TYPES

The tomato fruit is botanically classified as a berry. Cutting a standard round salad tomato in half transversely will show the fruit is made up of two, or in larger fruit, three sections (called 'locules'), divided by thin walls. The locules contain the seeds suspended in a type of jelly. These types of fruit are called bi-locular or tri-locular, and are the most familiar fruit type.

Cutting a beefsteak or canning plum tomato in a similar fashion will show that the fruit consists of many smaller locules, the dividing walls are much thicker, and the space for seeds and jelly much reduced: this is called a multi-locular fruit, and is the type preferred for canning and processing as it is firmer and contains more actual 'flesh' than the two locule types; it also cooks down to a firm paste.

Fruit shape can be anything from round to elongated, and size from tiny cherry-fruited to monsters weighing in excess of 500g (17oz).

The following are the main fruit types that are recognized commercially:

Beefsteak: The largest type in regular commercial production, the name 'beefsteak' originated in the USA, being the brand name that Anderson and Campbell (the first company to can tomatoes, starting in 1869) adopted for their first canned tomato product, which actually consisted of one single enormous tomato per can. These large, ridged, irregularly shaped fruit were sometimes known as 'cushion' tomatoes, and are many people's idea of what an old-fashioned tomato should look like. Modern commercial beefsteak-type tomatoes sold fresh weigh 170–280g (6–10oz), but there are varieties that regularly produce fruit of over 500g (17oz). The world record for the heaviest tomato is held by a monster beefsteak type produced in Oklahoma in 1986, which weighed in at 3.51kg (7lb 12oz)!

Plum-fruited: A distinction needs to be drawn here between the plum-fruited canning tomatoes, grown on determinate plants, and the plum-fruited tomatoes grown on indeterminate plants

Multi-locular fruit.

and sold fresh. The indeterminate types yielding plum-shaped fruit are a relatively new addition to the mainstream market. This category also includes the small-fruited cherry plum or baby plum types, which are often sold vine ripe.

Cherry-fruited: This type has a fruit weight between 10 and 25g (0.3 and 0.8oz), usually produced on long trusses. Modern commercial cherry tomatoes are often the 'vine-ripe' type, and sold as an entire truss.

Round-fruited: This is the standard familiar salad tomato weighing 70–110g (2.5–4oz – for the UK and US market, six to eight fruit to the pound), sometimes sub-divided into small round and large round types.

Pear-fruited: These are amongst the earliest known types of tomato (the varieties 'Red Pear' and 'Yellow Pear' are two of the oldest varieties still around), but have never been produced on any sort of scale. Recently some miniature pear-fruited types intended for vine-ripe production have been introduced.

There are plenty of other types of tomato that differ in shape, colour or both from those mentioned above.

Fruit Colour

Considering that the first tomatoes available in Europe were yellow fruited, it appears a bit odd that the red-fruited form came to dominate the

market for so many years – and continues to do so. Many colours are available in the tomato, the fruit colour depending on the content of various carotene pigments; in the majority the ratio of the prominent pigments lycopene (red) to beta-carotenes (yellow-orange) dictates the shade of red. Yellow tomatoes lack the lycopene pigment; the beta-carotene and other carotenes present dictate whether it is bright yellow or yellow/orange. The rather unusual white tomatoes have flesh that is very pale yellow, which looks white through the translucent skin of the fruit. Similarly pink tomatoes have red flesh and a translucent skin.

Whether one colour of tomato has any nutritional benefit over any other colour is debatable, though recent research has indicated that a form of lycopene found in orange-coloured tomatoes is more easily absorbed than the form that is dominant in the red-fruited types.

Vine Ripe?

For many years the standard way of harvesting salad tomatoes in Europe was to pick them a little bit under-ripe – at the orange rather than the fully red stage. This allowed a reasonable shelf life, and as the fruit was firmer at harvest it would suffer less damage in transit. Many people will remember the days of the first English home-produced tomatoes arriving in the shops looking a rather poor shade of orange.

Plant breeding led to the introduction of 'vine-ripe' types in the early 1990s, where the fruit could be harvested fully red-ripe and still have an acceptable shelf life.

This allowed the practice of harvesting 'on the vine', where the fruit could be left until an entire truss was ripe, and then the whole truss of fruit snipped off – this dramatically reduced harvesting time, particularly for the cherry-fruited types, and was instrumental in cherry-fruited types becoming a commercially viable crop.

Vine-ripe cherry plum tomatoes as harvested.

WHICH TYPES DO YOU GROW?

To many people, growing your own means producing something a little different to what can be found every day, but it depends on your priorities. Obviously there will be more choice for those who wish to raise their own plants, join a seed exchange, or search out the unusual from tomato enthusiasts, than for those who just want some nice red home-grown tomatoes, and purchase their plants from the local garden centre.

Determinate or Indeterminate?

For greenhouse or polytunnel cropping, the indeterminate types are the preferred choice as they keep on cropping reliably through a long season. For outdoor cropping, and with a planting date sometime in May, then both types have their own merits. Indeterminate types generally do not grow or set fruit particularly well at low temperatures, so a cool early summer will mean a slow start with delayed fruiting, but providing the late blight stays away, plants will continue fruiting right up until the first frosts. They need staking or supporting, and regular removal of the sideshoots.

Determinate or bush tomatoes tend to develop more quickly and to fruit earlier from a May planting, particularly if early summer conditions are cool. Because of their compact growth habit they are easier to protect with fleece or polythene early in the season. They have a spreading growth habit but do not need the same amount of maintenance (in terms of sideshoot removal and training) as the indeterminate types, which can be useful for allotment growers who can only get to their plots at weekends. On the down side they can be reluctant to continue fruiting late into the season, and the early fruit is often the best quality.

Semi-determinates can give the best or possibly worst of both worlds: they tend to fruit earlier than the indeterminates, but like the determinate types do not continue fruiting well into late season. The grower has the option of treating them as a determinate type and growing them as a large bush plant, or restricting them to a single stem by severe pruning of the lateral growth, which gives a fairly short plant with early fruiting capacity that can be useful in pots or where space is restricted.

If space permits it is worth experimenting with all types, trying some determinate tomatoes for early fruiting, and indeterminates for mid- and late summer.

F1 Hybrids

The first F1 hybrid tomato, named 'Fordhook Hybrid', was introduced in 1945 by the famous American seed company W. Atlee Burpee. The development came about as the company were making efforts to improve the quality and yield of home garden vegetables in response to the US government's Victory Gardens initiative.

To many people browsing the seed stand at the local garden centre the term 'F1 hybrid' is just a peculiar way of saying 'expensive'. Certainly with tomatoes, hybrid varieties are a great deal more costly than non-hybrid (technically called 'open pollinated') types – so what advantages do you get for your money?

Generally speaking, F1 hybrids outdo their open pollinated cousins in terms of vigour, which manifests itself in speed of growth and cropping capacity, and also uniformity, with all plants growing and developing at a similar rate and fruiting at the same time. Also in creating F1 hybrids, plant breeders can combine several disease resistance factors into one cultivar, which is well worth having. By comparison few of the open pollinated cultivars contain much in the way of inbuilt disease resistance.

Are F1 hybrids worth it? Generally yes, and for those not looking for anything too specific but who just want to grow a reliable crop of tomatoes with the least amount of trouble, the advantages F1 hybrids give are worth the extra money – besides which, for the number of plants the average back garden grower needs, the extra cost is hardly significant.

Just one caveat – growers cannot successfully save their own seed from F1 hybrids, as they will not come true to type – which is one of the reasons they are expensive.

Award Winners

Be a bit wary of terms such as 'prize winning' or 'gold medal', which are largely meaningless; but any variety that has received a Royal Horticultural Society Award of Garden Merit (AGM), or has a mention in the All America Selections (AAS), has been extensively evaluated by teams of independent experts.

SOME TOMATOES TO CONSIDER

Variety or Cultivar?

Both terms are in common use; strictly speaking a cultivar, which is short for CULTIvated VARiety, is something that has come about as a result of human interference, whereas a variety may have arisen naturally. Bearing in mind there are over 500 cultivars of tomato worldwide, this list is not intended to be extensive. It is also assuming average UK growing conditions, and includes both some easily available cultivars and some that may be more difficult to find.

Bush or Determinate Types

Unfortunately bush tomatoes can get overlooked by the 'mainstream' gardening market in that not

The very versatile 'Roma' grown in the highlands of Tanzania and packed ready for market.

all garden centres carry plants, and the seed of some cultivars can take a bit of seeking out.

'Roma': About the best known of the bush tomatoes is the cultivar 'Roma' (and its improved disease-resistant cousin 'Roma VF'), a name suggesting Italian origins, but actually developed by the United States Department of Agriculture (USDA) in 1955. This is the classic plum-shaped canning tomato with thick-walled fruits. Like all processing tomatoes, it is intended for a once-over mechanical harvest, so the ripe fruit remains in good condition when left on the plant. It is not the best tomato to be eaten fresh as the skin can be a bit tough, but it is very good grilled or fried, and excellent for sauces.

This cultivar has proved itself to be very adaptable to different climatic conditions, and is grown in many countries.

'Legend': For a modern bush cultivar, the large, round-fruited 'Legend', which was bred at Oregon State University and introduced on to the market in 2003 (also winning an RHS AGM), is very useful as it is tolerant of late blight, essential for the allotment environment. If trying this variety it is worth either mulching the plants with straw or providing some short canes for support in order to keep the heavyweight fruit off the soil. When grown as outdoor crops, few if any other cultivars will give enormous red multi-locular fruits as early in the season as 'Legend'.

'Sub-Arctic Plenty' and **'Sub-Arctic Maxi':** Two Canadian-bred cultivars intended for the short summer growing season of Greenland. They are famous for fruiting in the shortest possible time, and also setting fruit under cold conditions (these plants are parthenocarpic, meaning they are capable of setting fruit without the flowers being pollinated – a trait that is not common in the tomato, but occasionally shows up). The fruit is large cherry/standard round-sized, and if harvested just a little under ripe (to stop the slugs getting to it) it ripens well off the plant and keeps in good condition for a long time. If sown as a late outdoor crop these can reliably produce fruit into October, providing the frosts keep away.

'Whippersnapper': The seed might take a bit of seeking out, but this is a genuine, very small bush type rather than a novelty, with large cherry fruits, which are pink rather than red. Small enough to go into a hanging basket, though probably too big for a windowsill pot, it is mentioned here as it is about the earliest fruiting of the bush types.

'Green Sausage': An unusual cultivar, this plant has unique feathery foliage, and the fruits, as the name suggests, are sausage-shaped, elongated and striped dark/light green. They eventually turn yellow/green when fully ripe, but are best eaten at the immature green stage.

'Sweet Olive F1': A recent AGM winner, and a plant that falls into the 'intermediate' or semi-determinate category in that it will need stakes or canes for support, but does not need the regular sideshooting of the indeterminate types. The red fruit is olive-sized and shaped, and the plant crops well into the late season.

Indeterminate or Cordon Types

Cherry-Fruited Types

A favourite of the gardener long before they became commercially available, cherry-fruited types are usually very prolific in fruiting and easy to grow. For outdoor crops they have the advantage of being slightly earlier to ripen than the larger-fruited types, and also suffer less from fruit disorders such as cracking and blossom end rot. Cherry-fruited tomatoes tend to be more popular with children as they are usually sweeter than other types; the first three places in the British Tomato Growers Association's tastiest tomato competition of 2007 were taken by cherry-fruited cultivars.

'Sweet 100': For a red-fruited cherry type, 'Sweet 100' and its derivatives 'Supersweet 100' and 'Sweet Million' always look attractive with their

An autumn crop of the bush cultivar 'Sub-Arctic Plenty'; the cooler conditions seem to help the fruit quality.

extremely long fruit trusses. 'Sweet 100' is also particularly high in vitamin C, whether by accident or design.

'Ruby': An F1 hybrid that seems to do well as an outdoor subject; it crops well into the late summer/early autumn.

'Gardener's Delight': A red-fruited, open-pollinated cultivar that is considered to be fairly close to what the Victorians grew; it is also well known for flavour. The fruit occupies a borderline area between a large cherry and a small round. It gained AGM in 1997.

'Green Sausage'.

ABOVE: Ripening truss of the cherry tomato 'Ruby'.

BELOW RIGHT: Cherry tomato 'Sungold' grown as a multi-stemmed plant by allowing some sideshoots to develop. If grown as a single stem it can get very tall indeed.

Those who like 'Gardener's Delight' and want something slightly unusual should seek out the 'Del' series from specialist seed suppliers; these colourful fruited varieties were bred in the UK from 'Gardener's Delight' parentage, but never quite gained the same popularity as the original.

'Floridity F1': Has unusually shaped fruit, described as a mini plum type; it is high yielding, and crops well late in the season.

'Sungold': For yellow fruit 'Sungold' is well known for flavour, consistently performing well in taste tests. It also has a very thin skin, which children seem to prefer. Possibly because of this it does have an annoying habit of splitting its skin when picked fully ripe, so the trick is to harvest it just a little under-ripe, and leave it a couple of days in a bowl to ripen off.

'Sungold' holds the record for the longest tomato plant grown in the UK. In the year 2000 a 'Sungold' plant was grown to 19.8m (65ft) in length.

'Ildi': A unique yellow-fruited cultivar, with huge, multi-branched, bunch of grapes-style trusses of tiny, plum-shaped yellow fruit; the fruit seems to be of a better flavour if eaten slightly under-ripe at a light yellow colour, losing sharpness if allowed to ripen to deep yellow.

Lycopersicon pimpinellifolium: For something really old and unusual, track down some seed of the redcurrant tomato *Lycopersicon pimpinellifolium* from specialist suppliers on the internet, and grow it as early gardeners would have done, letting it scramble over a fence or trellis without any form of training.

'Balconi Red' and **'Balconi Yellow':** These miniature cultivars produce cherry tomatoes on plants so tiny they can be used as table decorations.

Round-Fruited Types

'Ailsa Craig': Of the old cultivars, 'Ailsa Craig', bred in Ayrshire in the late 1800s and still going strong, has a loyal following; it fruits well when grown as an outdoor crop, and appears generally reliable and trouble free.

'Moneymaker': Another well known old commercial cultivar originating in the UK; the big advantage of Moneymaker, and which accounted for its popularity when it was introduced in the 1950s, was that the fruits are free of 'greenback' disorder, still rampant amongst the opposition at the time. This variety has been derided occasionally in the popular UK press as being a prime example of the modern tasteless tomato, which is rather odd, because although very widely grown in the late 1950s and 1960s, it hasn't been a commercial variety in the UK for many years.

Despite having no genetic resistance to soil-borne diseases, the plant seems to be extremely tough, and has proved reliable under glass or outdoors, in soil or in growbags; it is also adaptable to many environments, and is a popular choice for smallholder farmers in the Kenyan highlands.

'Shirley': Of the more modern cultivars, the F1 hybrid 'Shirley' has made the transition from being a commercial greenhouse variety to a popular back-garden subject. It has compact growth with short internodes – quite unusual in modern commercial varieties – so is particularly well suited to the small greenhouse where height may be lacking. It fruits very reliably, with the fruit being of a consistent size and quality. It does well soil-grown, and has resistance to many soil-borne diseases. It gained an AGM in 1993.

'Vanessa': A modern F1 hybrid cultivar grown commercially and showing plenty of potential as a garden variety; it gained an AGM in 1997. Round-fruited, it is dual purpose as the fruit can be harvested on trusses as vine-ripe, or just picked conventionally. Trusses picked at the very end of the season will store for a number of weeks.

The stripy-fruited 'Tigerella'.

'Tigerella': For a slightly unusual round tomato, 'Tigerella' with its striped fruit looks a little different from the typical. It received an AGM in 1993.

'Ferline F1': One for the allotment – tomatoes suffer a number of disorders that also afflict potatoes, particularly 'late blight' caused by the fungus *Phytopthora infestans*. Ideally tomatoes and potatoes should not be in close proximity, as late blight often spreads from potatoes, hitting tomato plants in late August just when they are fruiting well. Unfortunately on an allotment it is rare to be more than a few yards from a crop of potatoes. 'Ferline' offers some resistance to late blight, which gives a measure of security – it will often succeed where others fail.

Beefsteak Types

'Brandywine': When discussing beefsteak tomatoes, particularly heritage types, the American variety 'Brandywine' soon crops up. Selected by nineteenth-century Amish farmers and named after a local creek, it is a great sprawling 'potato-leaved' variety, somewhat disease prone and difficult to train, throwing out massive sideshoots. UK growers who have tried 'Brandywine' have sometimes been disappointed by its performance – it seems to prefer the heat, and in a cool summer doesn't develop the intensity of flavour for which it is famous.

Young plants of 'Brandywine' showing the unusual potato-leaved foliage.

Some UK growers also find other beefsteak types rather disappointing when grown outdoors, although a lot depends on the nature of the summer. Fruits can be slow to ripen and prone to splitting. In the UK the following policy is suggested for beefsteak types:

- Use a stake for support rather than a string; once the plant develops fruit it gets very heavy, and strings can cut into the stem.
- 'Stop' the plant sooner than other types; these tomatoes are suited to longer summers than the UK delivers. Settle for fewer but better tomatoes.
- Truss prune to restrict the number of fruit, and put an extra tie on the stem above each truss or there is the danger of the fruit truss breaking off under its own weight.
- Don't be surprised if the earliest fruit is extra bumpy – low early season temperatures encourage very irregularly shaped fruit.

- Both cultivars listed below are widely available, have a successful track record in the UK, and have received an RHS AGM.

'Super Marmande': Originates from France, and is listed as either an indeterminate or semi-determinate cultivar according to the seed supplier – which is a bit arbitrary, since whichever category it falls into, it needs a hefty support because of the weight of the fruit. Typically it has large, flattened, ribbed fruit, and is usually reliable under UK conditions.

'Costoluto Fiorentino': An Italian heirloom variety, this plant is fairly compact with short internodes, and not as vigorous as other beefsteak types. The fruit is medium-sized and ripens fairly quickly in comparison to other cultivars.

A QUESTION OF TASTE

'Why don't tomatoes taste like they used to?' is an often heard complaint – everybody seems to remember that the tomatoes that came straight off the plant in Grandma's garden some dim and distant summertime past were infinitely superior in flavour to the ones they bought in a supermarket in November and kept in the fridge for a few days. Although it is easy to blame plant breeders for neglecting taste in favour of tonnage, it has to be remembered that the taste of the tomato relies on three factors:

'Super Marmande': like many beefsteak types the fruit is a little prone to cracking.

- The tomato itself, and its content of sugars, acids and aromatic compounds
- The growing method – conditions, irrigation and nutrition
- How the tomato is treated post harvest – from when it leaves the plant to when it gets to you, and also the amount of time it remains in the distribution process: like many fruits and vegetables, the sugar content of the tomato decreases with storage.

The Tomato Itself

Regarding the tomato itself, there are varieties that seem to crop up regularly in any taste tests and are listed amongst the personal favourites of keen tomato growers: for example in the UK 'Sungold' and 'Sweet 100' always seem to figure, whereas in the USA 'Celebrity' and 'Early Girl' have a faithful following.

The fruit type of the tomato has some bearing on the sweetness or sharpness of the fruit; the flesh of the tomato contains the most sugar, whereas the gel surrounding the seeds contains the most acid. When biting into a tomato the acidity is tasted before the sweetness, so because the two- or three-locular fruit types most commonly grown in the UK contain proportionally more gel than the larger multi-locular types, they tend to taste sharper.

Growing Conditions

Some years ago, trials took place at the UK's Glasshouse Crops Research Institute into how growing conditions affected the taste of tomatoes. The guinea-pig variety was the old favourite 'Gardener's Delight', which is generally recognized as a tasty tomato in the first instance. In summary, it was found that to grow a tomato with the best combination of high sugar combined with high acid levels for flavour, the main things a grower could do was to grow the crop fairly dry and to use high potassium feed once fruit development started.

This all seems fairly simple, but a limited watering regime can be hard to achieve in pots or growbags (though is somewhat easier with soil-grown greenhouse crops) if time restrictions mean watering can only be done once a day. Tomatoes do not appreciate a wet/dry cycling of the root environment and often respond with fruit splitting.

Post Harvest

Pick tomatoes as needed, and once harvested never put tomatoes into a refrigerator – this kills the production of the aromatic compounds, which are an important component of flavour. Under-ripe tomatoes will ripen more quickly and to no ill effect if kept in a paper bag with the top folded down.

TOMATO BREEDING AND DEVELOPMENT

Interestingly plant breeders are still returning to the so-called wild or *Eriopersicon* forms of tomato for genetic material when looking to improve characteristics for cultivation. Very conveniently these are all capable of hybridizing with *Eulycopersicon* types, and many commercial varieties owe part of their inbuilt resistance to disease to material donated by a wild relative. *Lycopersicon pennellii* is of current interest because of its strong root system and ability to survive on very little water, and a recent introduction has used parent material from the wild tomato *Lycopersicon cheesmanii*, a native of the Galapagos Islands, in its development.

Many tomato cultivars are not commonly available because they have been bred or selected for specific purposes, and are of little or no interest to a wider market. For example, the Campbell Soup Company and H. J. Heinz in the USA have developed a number of cultivars specifically for processing.

Selection and Adaptation

Many tomato cultivars were developed by the common man by the simple process of selection. The tomato is obligingly self-pollinating in that it does not require pollen from a separate plant in order to set seed, and consequently remains largely true to type. Farmers and gardeners who save their own seed have always selected the best performing plants to provide seed for next season, and the tomato helps the process, as one fruit can contain up to 200 seeds. Plants raised from these seeds have the best performers selected once again, and in three generations the plants come largely 'true to type'.

Bearing in mind that all tomatoes grown outside South America started life as imports at some point, over the years plants have been selected for best performance under local climate conditions and so become 'locally adapted' to warmer, cooler, drier, wetter, coastal or moun-

tainous regions. Taking the UK as an example, tomatoes were first grown as an outdoor crop, so quick-ripening types were needed in order to succeed in the relatively short season. Generally speaking, the smaller, round-fruited bi-locular types ripen in a shorter season than the larger-fruited multi-locular types, so selection tended to concentrate on these. Also the small fruited types tend to have anthers, which form a complete cone around the stigma and style, leading to more reliable self-pollination particularly in colder conditions. As a consequence the type of tomato developed for production in the UK, and still the most familiar to both growers and consumers, is the small/medium round bi-locular fruited type.

Although frequently cited by organic growers in the UK as important to biodiversity, the importance of maintaining locally adapted varieties is perhaps better recognized in countries where the climate and terrain vary considerably, and where most of the production is done by small farmers. In Kenya and Tanzania, for example, it is considered that 80 per cent of the crops grown by small and subsistence farmers come from the 'informal' seed market of home-saved seed and seed traded between neighbours.

Seed Savers, Heritage and Heirloom Varieties

Within the European Union, since the 1960s all vegetable varieties have been subject to the legal process of 'national listing' in order to be sold legally. To get a variety on to a national list requires a series of trials to assess whether the variety is distinct (not another variety masquerading under a different name), uniform and stable (DUS), and also has value for cultivation and use (VCU). Obviously costs are associated with this process, so for seed companies, only the more mainstream and popular varieties justify the

Seed of bush tomatoes and cabbage (amongst other things) on sale in a village market in Tanzania. Smallholders often interplant these two crops.

expense. Because of this, concern arose that many of the minor interest, locally adapted varieties would be lost because they could not be sold legally if they were not on the national list of a EU member state. As a consequence the seed saver networks came about.

The terms 'heritage' and 'heirloom' varieties essentially amount to the same thing: old, open-pollinated varieties that are no longer in commercial production. In America an heirloom variety is a variety that was available pre-1940. The varieties that are no longer supported by a seed company or plant breeder – and so, according to the letter of the law, can no longer be legally sold in Europe – are maintained and distributed by seed exchange networks, where no money is involved in the transactions so the seed is not actually 'sold'. This sidesteps the legislation.

Other varieties are supplied by recognized, often specialist seed companies who maintain old, interesting, non-mainstream varieties for the benefit of gardeners who like to grow something unusual. Both in the UK and in the USA there is much interest amongst the gardening public in these varieties, and plenty of discussion forums on the Internet. Furthermore, recognizing the need to preserve genetic material that may prove to be of value, the US Department of Agriculture has a seed library containing at least 5,000 tomatoes.

The purple-fruited tomato developed at the John Innes Centre.

GENETIC MODIFICATION (GM) AND THE TOMATO

A surprising number of people seem to think that most modern tomatoes, particularly anything of an unusual colour, are the result of GM technology. Why tomatoes attract this association is something of a mystery, though possibly the variety of fruit sizes, shapes and colours available looks almost too good and too diverse to have arisen naturally; also walking, talking tomatoes are an easy subject for cartoonists.

The fact of the matter is that, as far as market introductions go, GM technology hasn't gone very far with the tomato; possibly the experience of Calgene Fresh Inc. indicated that the public at large were not totally at ease with the idea. In 1994 Calgene launched their 'Flavr Savr' tomato, in which the gene responsible for causing the fruit to soften as it ripens had been 'turned off' or deactivated, so the ripe fruit remained firm for longer. Cans of tomato purée made from this, and duly labelled as containing GM ingredients, appeared on the supermarket shelves, where (in the UK at least) they tended to remain. When Calgene was bought out in 1997 'Flavr Savr' was taken off the market.

In the UK, work at the John Innes Centre has transferred a gene for anthocyanin production from Antirrhinum into the tomato, resulting in a beautiful deep purple/almost black fruit. Packed with antioxidants, it is believed there is potential for this fruit as a 'functional food'.

3 THE HISTORY AND DEVELOPMENT OF TOMATO PRODUCTION

The popularity of the tomato is still increasing – over the past forty years the total world crop area has increased by 164 per cent, and the consumption of tomatoes by a staggering 314 per cent. Consumption still increases by an average of 3 per cent annually. The reasons behind this increase are many and varied, though increased availability is perhaps the most obvious. In recent years, awareness of the potential health benefits associated with tomatoes is a likely contributing factor to the continued annual increase.

The reason for the apparent anomalies between production area and consumption in these figures is due to steady increases in yield: we produce more tomatoes per unit area of land than ever before.

TOMATOES FOR PROCESSING

World production of processing tomatoes, which are grown as a field crop often on an extremely large scale, is somewhere between 25 and 36 million tonnes annually to fill the demand for canned tomatoes, sauces, paste, juices and the myriad of other products containing tomato.

For canning or processing the industry requires a particular type of tomato, with a high content of solids and little in the way of the seeds or jelly found in salad tomatoes. Processing tomatoes are produced on determinate or bush plants; the

cultivars used are mainly F1 hybrids bred with a high degree of disease resistance. The fruit are thick-skinned to stand mechanical handling, and the fruit on the plant ripens almost simultaneously to allow a once-over 'destructive' harvest.

The plants are established in the field by sowing the seed directly into the soil, or since the advent of F1 hybrids with their more costly seed, grown from transplants. The crop takes between five and six months from establishment to maturity, and is usually harvested when 90 per cent of the fruit is ripe.

SALAD TOMATOES

Although there is some outdoor or field production of salad tomatoes (which amounts to quite an industry in the states of Florida and California), the vast majority of fresh or salad tomatoes are grown under some type of structure to give protection from the elements and a controllable or partially controllable environment. Although the tomato shows itself to be very adaptable to differing climatic regions, it usually performs better as a protected crop, gaining big improvements in both yield and quality over outdoor crops.

In the UK and northern Europe, and to some extent in North America, the structure used for commercial tomato production is usually a large glass greenhouse equipped with a full heating system; this is because summers are short and the conditions for outdoor cropping unreliable, and being able to protect and heat the crop gives a

OPPOSITE: **Large-scale tomato plant propagation.**

number of options to extend the length of the cropping season.

In southern Europe and the Mediterranean region, Africa and Asia, sheet or film plastic-clad structures (often known as polytunnels) are used, the main function of these being to conserve water and provide some protection from the extremes of temperatures often encountered (very hot days followed by cold nights), or other weather extremes such as heavy rain.

Tomato Production in Greenhouses

The basic way tomato plants are treated in the greenhouse hasn't changed too much from the early days. Indeterminate cultivars are used, planted in rows, and trained by loosely twisting up a vertical string attached to an overhead wire (the wire being attached to the greenhouse framework). The plants themselves are restricted to a single stem by removal of all sideshoot growth.

One factor that needed addressing right from the early days was what to do when the plant became too tall for the greenhouse. Various training methods such as the 'Guernsey arch' and 'bobbin layering' (methods still used today) were evolved to accommodate the increasing length of the stem while keeping the top of the plant at a reasonable height to allow routine work. Eventually towards the end of the season the plant would be 'stopped', which meant removal of the growing point to curtail any further vegetative growth so the plant could put its energies into ripening the remaining fruit.

If the basic production method is still much the same as it was in the early days, one factor that has changed considerably is the length of the cropping season. For many years tomatoes under glass were treated as a seasonal crop, grown in rotation with other salads and cut flowers. In the UK, tomatoes could be grown as an early season heated crop, planted in late January and kept until about the end of July, when the crop would have realized most of its potential income (as most of the money was made on the early season fruit); it was then followed with cut flower chrysanthemums, which would crop from the autumn through until Christmas. Another approach was to plant the tomato crop in March, which incurred less of a heating bill than earlier plantings, keep the crop right through the summer, then follow with a crop of winter lettuce.

With developments in greenhouse technology and the need to intensify production, the season for tomato crops began to extend, starting earlier and finishing later in the year. This has developed to such an extent that in northern Europe and the UK, mainstream tomato production has become an increasingly specialist operation. Seasonal tomato production is very much reduced, and

TOP: 'Moneymaker' tomato planted in a polytunnel on a Kenyan farm. Plastic mulch is used for water conservation.

BELOW: A commercial tomato crop; the plants are supported by strings suspended from a top wire.

A young plant propagated in a cube of rockwool.

Tomatoes in the UK

'Guernsey Toms'

Historically the island of Guernsey is the traditional supplier of tomatoes (the famous 'Guernsey Tom') to mainland UK. Production of tomatoes started in a small way, and when they were first adopted as a major crop (round about the mid-1880s), the growers already had some twenty years' experience in tomato growing so the industry was able to develop rapidly.

How the Guernsey growers gained their initial experience with the tomato crop was due to a 'spin-off' from the production of one of the island's main horticultural exports. From 1850 there had been a major expansion of the greenhouse industry as very good money could be made producing table grapes for the mainland market. Traditional Guernsey greenhouses were (and still are) known as vineries, impressive wood-framed structures built to a very high standard by the island's shipbuilders.

As the cultivation method chosen for grape vines left some vacant growing space in the centre of the vinery, tomatoes started to be grown as a

most tomatoes are grown as a monocrop, which means the nursery just produces tomatoes, and no other crop. The only break in cropping comes when one crop is cleared out and a new one started. It also concentrates 100 per cent on production: plants are bought in from specialist raisers rather than propagated on site.

The usual approach is a long season crop, which requires a fully heated greenhouse as the plants are put into the production house just before Christmas, and then taken through until about the end of October, giving 6–8 weeks to clear out the old crop, do various maintenance tasks and set up for the new crop. This method gives fruit from March to October.

A second approach that has evolved in more recent years is to produce the crop year round, so filling the winter production gap. This can only be done in the most modern greenhouses equipped with artificial lighting as well as highly efficient heating systems to give adequate growth and cropping during the dark winter months.

TOMATOES ON SEA

Maritime environments are preferred for greenhouses as the milder winter climate reduces fuel requirement, and the sea breezes and cooler summer temperatures mean there are fewer problems with excessively high temperatures under glass in the summer.

Add to this the average 1,800 hours of sunshine a year, and Guernsey has a winning combination.

Much of the UK mainland glasshouse industry developed in coastal districts, particularly the south coast, and the industries in southern Spain and in the Canary Islands also benefit from the relative climatic stability provided by the proximity of the sea.

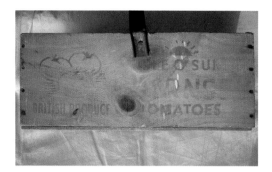

An 'Isle o' Sun' tomato box or 'chip', in which the famous Guernsey Tom came to the mainland.

'catch crop' or additional crop to make profitable use of these spaces. Gradually the idea caught on, until tomatoes started to be grown as a main crop in their own right. Soon tomato exports were also making good money: in 1887 1,000 tons of Guernsey tomatoes sold for £30,000 on the mainland, a figure that would equate to about £2,650 per ton today.

Grape production on Guernsey peaked in about 1915, after which the island became a major producer of tomatoes supplying the mainland. In the high season, special 'tomato trains' would run from Weymouth to London to cope with the tonnage imported. By the 1960s the greenhouse industry on the island had grown to such an extent that further expansion was curtailed by law.

Tomatoes on the UK Mainland

Tomatoes were not produced in any sort of commercial quantity until about 1870, after which the newly emerging commercial greenhouse industry started to adopt the crop quite rapidly.

The big boost to tomato production came during World War II. Greenhouses were nearly all put over to food crop production (although flower growers were allowed to keep 10 per cent of their 1939 production area in order to preserve stock material), and by 1942 tomatoes were the summer crop in the majority of greenhouses. In 1946, which was about the peak year for home production of food crops, the UK mainland had a staggering 1,416ha (3,500 acres) of greenhouse tomatoes, and a further 1,821ha (4,500 acres) of outdoor tomato crops. Following this there was a rapid decline in production area, and by 1962 the commercial production of outdoor tomatoes on the UK mainland had all but ceased.

In more recent years, with improved transport and the need for suitable soils being negated by changes in production method, the UK greenhouse industry has moved away from the traditional areas of its beginnings, although much tomato production still takes place south of the Thames due to the better winter light conditions.

Total UK commercial production, all greenhouse grown, is around 75,000 metric tonnes per year, which only partially satisfies the UK's appetite, accounting for about a quarter of the fresh tomatoes sold in the UK annually.

Imports from the Netherlands

Though having a well developed greenhouse industry providing a range of crops, the Dutch took to tomato production somewhat later than the English. Regular shipments of fruit and vegetables from the Netherlands to the UK had started in the 1820s, but it wasn't until nearly 100 years later that Dutch tomatoes became a significant import to the UK.

By 1960 the Netherlands had over 5,000ha (12,355 acres) of greenhouses, with 75 per cent of this area producing tomatoes. In more recent years the Dutch tomato industry has contracted a little in the face of competition from southern Europe; many tomato growers changed to sweet pepper (*Capsicum*) production as an alternative, and those who remained with tomatoes now tend to grow vine-ripe, cherry and the more 'specialist' types and leave the production of the standard round tomato to the competition. The Dutch still have around 1,370ha (3,385 acres) of glass producing tomatoes, with Germany as its main customer.

The Dutch remain the leaders in all aspects of greenhouse technology, from the design of the structures and the environmental control systems to the machines which grade and pack tomatoes.

A glasshouse crop of sweet pepper or capsicum; the production method used is similar to that used for tomato.

A New Industry in Spain

Since the 1970s major developments in the south of Spain (Almeria and Murcia regions) have resulted in a vast area – nearly 54,000ha (133,434 acres) – of 'plasiculturas': fairly unsophisticated plastic-clad greenhouses producing a wide range of fruit and vegetable crops for export mainly during the northern European winter. Tomato production in these regions takes place in the 'off' season for northern Europe, between September and May.

What Future for the Greenhouse Tomato Crop?

Questions are sometimes asked about the validity of growing an essentially tropical crop year round in latitudes where such a high input of energy is involved, but the alternative of importing the fruit from warmer climes also uses considerable energy. The current trend for tomato production in the UK and Europe is to grow the crop on an extremely large scale, so benefiting from the economies of scale.

Amongst the challenges facing the industry, fuel and labour costs figure very highly, though greenhouse cropping in general is adopting new technologies and using waste heat and new fuels. Development work in the USA has shown potential for a radical departure from the European method of crop production. Tomato plants are grown at a high density (eleven plants per m^2) on benches, and allowed to produce just one truss of fruit. Once this is harvested the plants are discarded and replaced with new, and the whole process repeated. By this method up to five crops per year are produced.

The advantages to this system are that the labour for hands-on operations such as trimming and training is not needed, plants grown on benches can be rolled in front of pickers, or the possible next development is to mechanize the process and have the fruit picked by robots!

4 PLANT RAISING

To many people, plant raising is the difficult, fiddly bit of the growing operation, and as most gardeners don't need so many tomato plants – one American source states that two plants per adult are needed to supply the household with fruit through the summer – it is frequently a great deal simpler to buy plants than raise them.

Bought-in plants can restrict a grower to the more mainstream varieties, particularly if buying from the larger 'chain' garden centres; via the internet it is possible to source a much wider range, though on-line plant sales tend to supply small plants otherwise postage costs can be prohibitive. From Easter onwards every car boot sale will have someone offering tomato plants, but the quality can leave something to be desired.

If specific or unusual varieties are required, or to maintain quality control over the whole process, there is only one answer: grow your own. And it's not difficult at all!

PLANT RAISING FROM SEED

Where many people come unstuck with plant raising is by starting too early and growing too many, with the result that in late April every windowsill in the house is crammed with plants waiting for the weather to improve. Tomato seed will keep for a couple of years providing some basic rules are followed, and germination is fairly reliable, so if only five plants are required there is no need to sow the whole packet.

OPPOSITE: **Seedling propagation on the kitchen windowsill. Turn the pot round daily as the seedlings will grow towards the light.**

Assuming plants are intended for the earliest possible plantings, which requires a sowing date in February/March, and also assuming the seeds will be sown indoors and plants raised on windowsills or in a heated conservatory, then 10–13 weeks should be allowed from sowing to planting. Proceed as follows:

- Equip yourself with some suitable containers. For small-scale sowings of up to twenty seeds, small plant pots are better than seed trays as they take up less room and, being considerably deeper than trays, allow deeper rooting.
- Use proprietary seed compost: there are plenty on the market, but a good rule to remember is that regarding quality of product, you usually get what you pay for.
- Fill the pot, press the surface down flat, leaving at least 10mm (⅜in) below the rim – it's worth spending a minute or two getting this right and giving a perfectly flat surface.
- Tomato seed is large enough to be space sown; however, the seed does differ considerably in physical size, thus tiny cherry tomatoes have tiny seeds.
- Tip the seeds out on to a piece of paper and examine them – tear the packet open completely as seeds often get stuck in corners; they also have a tendency to stick together, so be sure to separate them. F1 hybrid seeds are usually sold by count, so if it looks as if the packet is a few short of the number promised, probably some are stuck together.
- Space the seeds evenly on to the compost surface; they can be shuffled around using the point of a small knife, if needs be. Use the whole area available.

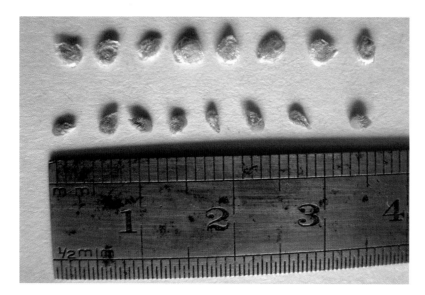

LEFT: **The variation in tomato seed size; cherry-fruited at the bottom.**

BELOW: **Seed sowing in a 9cm pot.**

- Cover the seeds with a comparatively thick layer of compost 5mm (¼in) or so deep – this is to make sure the seed coat is entirely removed as the emerging growth pushes through the covering. Perlite or vermiculite is sometimes preferred as covering media.
- The next operation is to water – unless this is done very carefully there is a good chance of upsetting all the careful work done so far. The preferred method is to stand the pot in a bowl of water and let it soak for a few minutes so the surface is not disturbed. This will tend to

waterlog the compost initially, so let it drain afterwards.

GERMINATION

Germination now relies on temperature, so the container can be put somewhere warm regardless of light as long as it is checked daily for signs of germination.

Tomatoes need a temperature above 15°C for reliable germination; higher temperatures up to about 23°C can be employed if available, but check the containers regularly as there is an increased chance of the compost drying out. At lower temperatures (between 10° and 15°C) germination will happen, but will be severely delayed.

For anyone lacking a suitable source of heat for pots or trays of seeds, some UK-based research in the 1970s showed that if tomato seeds are pre-germinated at 21°–24°C, they can then be planted into compost and kept under cooler conditions (10°–15°C) and will still grow satisfactorily. This process involves germinating the seed in a suitably warm environment (say, next to the domestic hot water tank) on some dampened kitchen towel or similar until the root is just starting to emerge, then carefully (using tweezers) transferring the seeds to compost. If doing this, remember the seed will need checking daily and the seeds moving into compost as soon as germination occurs.

Small-Scale Plant Raising

Seed emergence. This is an open-pollinated cultivar so emergence occurs over several days. F1 hybrid types tend to germinate more evenly.

A 9cm pot and the top two-thirds of a plastic soft drinks bottle make a good combination for windowsill propagation.

Seedlings start to emerge in five to eight days depending on the temperature – if growing an F1 hybrid all seeds will germinate more or less together, whereas with open-pollinated types it may take a few days for all the seedlings to fully emerge.

All vegetable seed sold in the EU has to conform to minimum standards for germination; with tomato the figure is 75 per cent. F1 hybrid seeds usually germinate better than this, but work on the assumption that a packet of ten seeds will give eight plants.

The 2ltr (3.5-pint) 'greenhouse' and 9cm (3.5in) pot is a combination that could have been purposely designed with windowsill or small-scale plant raising in mind. If seeds are sown into 9cm (3.5in) round plastic pots (which have sufficient space to comfortably raise twenty or so seedlings to transplanting size), then it will be found that the top two-thirds of a 2ltr (3.5-pint) plastic soft drinks bottle is a snug fit over the pot. Leave the screw cap on the bottle initially as this will maintain the humidity and stop the surface of the pot drying out; remove the cap once the seedlings emerge.

These seedlings are at about the right stage for potting up; the roots may become difficult to separate if they are left to get any larger.

There is no great hurry to move the seedlings on to the next stage; providing they are not too crowded they can comfortably be left in the propagation pot until the cotyledons are fully expanded and the first true leaf is starting to appear.

From now on it is important to avoid the combination of too high a temperature with too little light: as well as producing thin, unhealthy-looking plants, the combination has other effects on the growth pattern of the plant, such as delaying the development of the first fruiting truss.

Checking for Sibling Plants

One slight flaw with F1 hybrid tomatoes is the unwelcome presence of a small percentage of plants known as siblings, or 'sibs'. When the F1 hybrid seed is created, two parent lines are cross-pollinated, and each seed should be a product of both parents (a hybrid). Unfortunately, as it can be difficult to stop tomatoes self-pollinating, there are usually a few seeds formed by one of the parent plants doing just that. This seed is not a hybrid as it has come from only one parent, so the plant will be substantially different to the hybrid plants. Sibs should not be used, as the chance of them producing any reasonable tomatoes is minimal.

Fortunately these 'sib' plants look very different from the hybrid plants from a very early age, showing as much smaller and often with twisted leaves, and amongst a group of utterly uniform F1 hybrid plants they obviously stand out. Luckily the percentage of 'sibs' in any batch of plants is low, and if you find one in a batch of ten, consider yourself unlucky.

RE-POTTING THE GROWING PLANTS

The seedlings now need moving on into individual containers. The size of pot used really depends on how much space is available. Young tomato plants seem very tolerant of re-potting operations so it is all right to put the plants into small-sized pots at this stage with the intention of moving them on again into the final pots a few weeks later. Commercial growers would put the seedlings into their final pots at this stage to save labour later on, but obviously larger pots take up more space.

Potting Compost

Whatever is decided regarding containers, a 'general purpose' potting compost is needed at this stage. There is quite an array of potting composts on the market, and it is possible to be spoilt for choice.

John Innes potting is a tried and trusted name – the recipes developed at the John Innes research institute in the 1950s were the first standardized composts used in horticulture. These are made in three different 'strengths', depending on the amount of fertilizer they contain; for tomato plants at this stage, John Innes potting No. 1 is the one to use.

What makes the JI mixes different from the great majority of composts around today is their bulk ingredients: they are based on sterilized loam, peat and grit. The loam content makes the compost very forgiving and tolerant of over- and under-watering – useful with small pots that are fiddly to water. It is also heavier than other types of compost so pots are less prone to tipping over as plants get taller. Plants in a JI compost will not need any supplementary feeding during the propagation stage.

Peat-based composts constitute the majority of composts on the market today, and again, you tend to get what you pay for. Although usually reliable, some peat-based composts can be a bit difficult to re-wet if they have been allowed to dry out. The cure for this is to stand the plants in a shallow bowl of water and let them soak for a couple of hours.

Peat-free composts can be somewhat variable in texture, depending on what ingredients have been used instead of peat. If any comparisons are to be made between the performance of peat-based and peat-free mixes, the peat-free mixes tend to be more freely draining and don't retain as much water as the peat-based types; this is particularly true of composts based on coir or 'cocofibre'. At the initial potting-up stage this is of only minor significance, but it is important to remember this as the plants get bigger and more demanding of water.

How to 'Pot Up'

Whichever compost you choose, there are a few general rules for potting tomato seedlings.

- Fill the pot completely, do not compact the compost, strike the surface level, and tap the pot on the table just to settle the compost.
- Make a deep hole in the centre.
- Extract a seedling holding it by one of the cotyledons: if this breaks, the plant will still survive – if you hold it by the stem and cause any damage, it won't.
- Bury the plant so the cotyledons are just fractionally above the compost surface – the reason for this is that tomato plants can put out roots all the way along the stem, so by burying the stem we encourage a bigger and better root system at an early stage of growth. Also it is quite possible that the seedlings will have grown fairly tall by this stage, particularly if grown on a windowsill or if they were a bit crowded in the propagation container.
- Water the plants thoroughly; often the cotyledons settle on to the surface of the compost, but this is nothing to worry about, and the plants grow out of it in a couple of days.

The aim now is to grow a sturdy and compact plant, which is achieved by getting the balance right between light and temperature; thin, pale,

ABOVE: **Good seedling root development; using a pot rather than a tray allows deeper rooting and less root tangling.**

BELOW LEFT: **Preparing for potting up; the size of pot used at this stage rather depends on how much propagation space is available.**

BELOW RIGHT: **If buried, the whole of this plant stem is capable of producing adventitious roots, giving the plant a more extensive root system.**

Seedling potted to the correct depth.

BIO-DEGRADABLE AND LATTICE POTS

These types of pot are worth considering for the final potting, particularly if the intention is to grow tomato plants in grow-bags.

Bio-degradable pots are made of a paper/peat or paper/coir mixture; at planting time the base of the pot is simply torn away and the entire pot dropped into the planting hole giving minimum root disturbance.

Lattice pots are often used for aquatic plants; the bottom third of the pot is made of a latticework of plastic. Once potted, the tomato roots soon hold the compost together stopping it leaking out through the latticework, then at planting time the whole pot is planted to the depth of the lattice. The result is no root disturbance followed by quick root emergence.

over-tall plants are a result of too little light. The rule at this stage is never to crowd the plants together, arrange plants in a single row along the windowsill, with space between each plant. When the leaves start to touch it is time to re-space.

GROWING ON

Use of 'Grow Lights'

These are used extensively in the commercial world for plant production in the early months of the year. Grow-light kits are available to the amateur, however the investment and running cost of these is only likely to be justified for those producing a large number of plants, and who have the facilities (such as a heated greenhouse or conservatory) to cope with these numbers as they grow larger. Lamps can, and do increase plant growth rate and improve quality, which are the main reasons for their adoption by commercial plant raisers, but there is little point in producing the healthiest plants too early for them to progress satisfactorily to the next growth stage.

Growing On in the Final Pot

On average an indeterminate tomato plant will produce seven or eight true leaves before producing the first truss of flowers, and during this stage there is not much that needs to be done. Some cultivars start producing sideshoots at an early stage, which should be removed as soon as they are large enough to get hold of comfortably between finger and thumb. Taller plants may need supporting using a small split cane and wire tie.

The Final Stage before Planting Out

If plants are getting too big for the final pot and conditions are not yet suitable for planting them out, then sometimes a bit of shock treatment is used, and this is no bad thing.

The first truss of flowers the plant produces is the most important to both the commercial and amateur grower. If the plant is put into its final growing position at too young a stage, it can go into a state of rapid vegetative growth, in which case the first truss is often aborted or sometimes doesn't appear at all. In commercial crops, to make sure the first truss appears and produces fruit, shock treatment is used.

Plants are kept in the propagation container until they are well and truly 'pot bound'; this puts them under stress and pushes them into reproductive rather than vegetative growth. As a rule the plant should not be moved on into its grow-bag or final planting position until the first flowers on the first truss are open, or at least showing some colour. By this stage the plants are usually getting too tall for the pot they are in and are prone to falling over, also the lower foliage may be losing colour as the plant runs out of nutrients; however, no long-term damage is caused, it makes sure that the early fruit is set, and once the plant is moved into the final planting position it soon recovers.

ABOVE: Sideshoot development starting on a young plant. These will need removing.

RIGHT: Shock treatment prior to planting; the plant is kept pot-bound until the flowers on the first truss are established.

5 HOUSING YOUR TOMATOES

GREENHOUSES

Small greenhouses have a reputation of being difficult to work with, which to an extent is true in that smaller structures are more prone to rapid temperature and humidity fluctuations than larger structures; however, all greenhouses have their limitations, and gardeners just need to be aware of them and to be prepared to work around them. For anyone wishing to invest in a greenhouse, the choice and variety of structure available to the gardener has never been greater; nevertheless, whatever type is being considered, whether it is a costly hand-crafted, traditional-style, wood-framed greenhouse or a budget-priced aluminium-framed structure, there are a couple of key things to remember when making comparisons:

- Greenhouse size is usually quoted in terms of area of ground covered, for example 1.8 × 2.4m (6 × 8ft), but for crops of tomatoes it is also important to consider the height to the eaves. A greenhouse crop of tomatoes will get tall, and if comparing greenhouses with crops of tomatoes in mind, go for the taller structure every time.
- Another feature to consider is ventilation area; as an example, a ventilation opening area equivalent to one sixth of the floor area is thought necessary for commercial green-

OPPOSITE: **A restored Victorian 'lean-to' greenhouse with tomatoes in the border soil against the wall, making the most of the tallest part of the structure and benefiting from the wall retaining heat overnight.**

houses. However, although the provision of opening vents obviously adds to the cost, some smaller budget-priced structures lack sufficient ventilation.

Other than these points the choice of structure is fairly open. 'Traditional' wood-framed structures always gain from the aesthetic point of view, and can make an excellent garden feature. The traditionally favoured wood for the frame of the small greenhouse is Western red cedar (from the tree *Thuja plicata*): it is expensive but rot and maintenance free, and looks superb. It is said that wood-framed structures can stay warmer than metal-framed ones, particularly if on a brick base, but in reality the difference is not appreciable.

Aluminium frames are perhaps more popular for smaller structures, being cheaper than wooden frames (particularly red cedar). Some manufacturers use a green coating on the aluminium, which makes it somewhat easier on the eye and blends into the garden better than shiny aluminium.

When siting a free-standing greenhouse, the site needs to be level; however, a compromise between shelter and shade is usually sought.

Old pictures of Victorian walled gardens often show 'lean-to' greenhouses against a wall, with tomatoes being grown in the bed next to the wall and trained up wires. There is a lot of good sense to this, and as well as considering a free-standing greenhouse, if there is potential for a lean-to structure against a suitable wall, this option is well worth looking into. Lean-to structures are excellent for tomatoes: as well as benefiting from extra height, they can stay warmer than free-standing houses because the wall heats up during the day and acts as a kind of storage radiator,

The greenhouse can provide valuable shelter from frost and pests for the growing plants.

releasing the heat overnight. Tomato plants trained against the wall directly benefit from this.

Greenhouse Glazing

On safety grounds, 4mm-thick toughened glass seems to be replacing the old standard 3mm horticultural glass, which is a good idea around the domestic environment. If safety glass is broken it shatters rather like a car windscreen, with no razor-edged shards.

The rigid plastic materials acrylic and polycarbonate are also popular from the safety point of view and because of their ability to stop a flying frisbee without damage, but they have other advantages as well: being much lighter in weight than glass they require less support, so larger panels can be used. Acrylic panels can be curved, leading to some manufacturers offering some very interesting curvilinear designs. Furthermore, an important factor for anyone considering heating a greenhouse is that both types of plastic offer a measure of insulation, something that glass does not do at all. Polycarbonate is often manufactured as two- or three-layer panels, and these give a type of 'double glazing' insulation effect,

which helps the structure retain heat when the sun goes in.

OTHER HOUSING

Polytunnels

Film-plastic houses, sometimes known as 'polytunnels', do not seem to have gained much popularity as garden structures, possibly because they are purely functional and lack the aesthetic appeal of a greenhouse. In comparison to glass or rigid plastic-glazed structures they are very much cheaper to buy and can be very versatile; however, an allowance has to be made for replacement of the plastic cover every three to five years.

If considering a polytunnel, again think about height: some structures lack height apart from in the very centre, which can be restricting. Designs which have vertical sides and a curved top are better for tomatoes than a straightforward hoop profile, though might cost a bit more. Polytunnels are known to get very humid and excessively hot in summer due to limited ventilation, but with smaller sizes this is less of an issue as the door provides sufficient ventilation. One well known disadvantage of polytunnels when compared with glasshouses is that they do not exhibit the 'greenhouse effect' and retain heat in the same way as a glasshouse.

The 'Keder' House

An interesting and quite unique structure is the 'Keder' house, which uses a film-plastic covering material resembling bubblewrap – but there the comparison ends, as this material is super tough and resists all attempts to pop the bubbles, even by the most determined child. Because of its structure the covering gives excellent heat-retaining properties due to its capacity for insulation, and also lasts a great deal longer than other film plastics. Originally developed as a commercial greenhouse, a variety of smaller garden-sized structures is available.

TEMPERATURE CONTROL IN THE GREENHOUSE

The extremes of temperature for tomato produc-tion are usually taken as 12°C and 30°C. Night temperatures below 12°C cause plants to effectively stand still, and day temperatures above 30°C put them under too much stress.

Early in the season some extra insulation can be employed to try and stop the night temperatures dropping too far. Either film plastic or bubblewrap can be attached to the internal structure to provide a double-glazed effect, but the greater the extent to which this is done, the more light is compromised. It is usual to treat the gable ends and about halfway up the sides, and to create a hanging curtain just inside the door, as this gives a reasonable compromise between insulation and light transmission.

In high summer keeping the temperature down can be a problem; there are various paints that can be applied to the outside of the glass, which reflect much of the light – the treatment is usually done on the roof only, as the main problem occurs when the sun is overhead. A less messy solution is to use shade netting over the roof in either a single or double layer, though it is important that this is fixed to avoid the roof ventilation

The 'Keder' house.

An electric greenhouse fan heater. This model uses a capillary expansion thermostat for accuracy.

This type of heater is small in size, easily movable and can be suspended to keep it out of the way, and the heat is instantly available. It is important to use a dedicated greenhouse heater designed for the job, and not court danger by improvising with a domestic alternative.

Greenhouse heaters are rated to standard IP21, which means they are safe for use in a damp environment; also dedicated greenhouse heaters are usually fitted with a more accurate thermostat than domestic heaters, which is important in order to keep the electricity bills down. If shopping for a fan heater it is also worth considering one with a 'cool air' ventilation option, where the fan can be used without heat: this is useful for shifting condensation first thing in the morning.

altogether – even a piece of netting will restrict the airflow. Shade netting can also be used on the inside, which looks neater though may be more troublesome to fix.

It is useful to obtain a piece of netting of a larger mesh size to make a door curtain, so the door can be left fully or partially open for extra midday ventilation. The mesh should be small enough to keep cats and inquisitive birds out, but large enough to allow pollinating insects in.

In today's environmentally sensitive times heating a greenhouse does take some justification even if the expense is not an issue. Most tomato growers who use artificial heat at all restrict themselves to a bit of heating early in the season at plant-raising time in order to prevent frost damage, and possibly to temper cold nights at the end of the season so that late crops of fruit suffer less splitting and disease damage. About 1.5kw capacity is needed for frost protection in an average-sized garden structure.

Electric Heaters

Where the power source is available, one of the simplest forms of heating suited to keeping the frost off the small greenhouse is the electric-powered warm-air fan heater.

Paraffin or LPG heaters

In some ways paraffin heaters are the traditional small greenhouse heater, and the choice for situations where electric power is not an option. Obviously these are not as controllable as electric heaters, though some designs do have thermostatic control.

The problem with burning paraffin or LPG in a closed environment such as a greenhouse is the amount of water vapour that is generated. In most small greenhouses there are usually plenty of air leaks even with the door and ventilators shut, but if efforts have been made to insulate the structure with a layer of film plastic or bubblewrap on the inside walls, then the atmosphere can get very humid.

Solar Heating

Maybe in the not-too-distant future more technological help will be at hand, as the price of solar panels comes down; certainly each generation of PV (photovoltaic) panels seems to double in efficiency compared to its predecessor – for example we now have panels that generate electricity in normal daylight rather than only in bright sunlight. A greenhouse that generates some of its own power for heating is a definite possibility.

WATER SUPPLY TO THE GREENHOUSE

It is important to consider where the water supply for the greenhouse will come from. Usually there is an outside tap on the house wall, but the greenhouse is often some distance away, and the novelty of lugging cans of water from the house soon wears off in a prolonged hot spell – obviously greenhouse-grown tomatoes will have a healthy rate of water consumption through the summer. If the greenhouse structure has provision for guttering, then it is well worth installing a water butt (or even two if room permits) to collect the roof water. Water butts need to be installed on firm supports of bricks/paving slabs and should be raised off the ground by about 60cm (2ft) so there is room to get watering cans under the taps. If the mains water supply is some distance away, then in dry weather the water butts can be topped up with a hose as a 'once a week' job, as a time saver for routine watering. This also has the advantage of giving the water time to warm up to ambient temperatures in the summer.

USING THE GREENHOUSE SOIL

In the not-too-distant past, the suitability of the local soil for the intended crops would have been a deciding factor in the siting of a greenhouse. In the garden a greenhouse is often just put on a base of slabs, and any potential of the soil underneath is ignored. This is reasonable, bearing in mind the site usually needs a bit of levelling, and putting down a solid base is the easiest way of doing it: if the soil is heavy clay, of an extreme pH, or something consisting largely of builders' rubble, it is often the least trouble to ignore it and grow all plants in containers – but if it is usable, there are considerable advantages in having it available.

Why Use the Soil?

Overall, tomatoes grown in the soil take the least amount of effort to look after:

- The plants manage themselves to a degree, and don't need a great deal of attention early in the season.
- Little major harm is done if watering and feeding are both a bit erratic, which can be important for anyone working irregular hours.
- Tomatoes in the soil will rarely suffer from water stress, which is all too common in containers and other media.
- Specific nutritional problems such as trace element deficiencies are usually very rare.
- Overall, fewer fertilizers are usually required.
- 'Grey water' can be used for irrigation purposes.
- Many are of the opinion that soil-grown tomatoes taste better.

The main problem encountered is long term, and caused by the need to plant tomatoes in approximately the same position each year.

Soil Sickness

From the earliest days of production right up until the late 1960s/early 1970s tomatoes were grown in the greenhouse soil (sometimes known as 'border soil', a hangover from the days when all planted areas of walled gardens were called borders regardless of what was grown), and great pains were taken to prepare the soil for this long season, rather hungry crop.

One problem that became apparent was that of 'soil sickness', which is a general term to describe the build-up of pests and diseases that can persist in the soil from one crop to the next. Tomatoes are very prone to a number of fungal diseases affecting the roots, and there are also two species of soil-living nematode or eelworm that cause significant root damage: if the soil cannot be given a sufficiently long break between crops for these pests and diseases to die (impractical in the commercial world), then the next planting of tomatoes will suffer badly.

From about 1902 the technique of soil sterilization by steam was developed: this involved injecting steam (generated by the greenhouse heating boilers) into the soil for several hours to sterilize or 'cook' it. Sometimes this had to be done annually between crops, and as can be imagined, it was a costly, unpleasant and labour-intensive business, and very unpopular with the workers – on larger nurseries it involved working day and night until the job was finished.

Growers realized that by using some other form of growth medium that was isolated from the soil, then disposing of it at the end of the crop, the major problem of pest and disease carry-over, and the need for sterilization with all its cost and inconvenience, could be avoided altogether. This was a major factor in bringing about the change to growing crops in isolated media, and the development of systems that are used by commercial growers today.

Problems with soil sickness can occur in the small greenhouse or even an outdoor area, in that putting any seasonal plant in the same position each year can lead to a build-up of pests and/or diseases specific to that plant, because there isn't enough time between crops for the pests/diseases to die off. The usual sign of soil sickness with tomatoes is a gradual reduction in yield due to poorer plant performance year on year. Early research in commercial greenhouses indicated that over four years the yield of soil-grown tomatoes can decrease by 27, 39, 50 and 67 per cent if the pathogens are allowed to build up unchecked. In extreme cases it becomes impossible to grow the plant in that situation.

Because it is valuable to be able to use the soil, it is worth considering the options for dealing with soil sickness.

Changing the Soil

Back in Victorian times the problems of soil sickness were known (though the causes were not fully understood), and when it occurred, the problem was dealt with by digging out the greenhouse soil to a depth of 90cm (3ft) or so, barrowing it away and replacing it with good quality garden soil from elsewhere. If this doesn't sound too much like hard work, and access to other cultivated ground is available, then digging the soil out of a greenhouse border and replacing it

---

ENARENADO

Tomato growers in the vast polytunnel nurseries in south-eastern Spain get round the dual problem of poor quality local soil and soil sickness by using an imported soil mixture known as 'Enarenado'. The local rocky, sandy soil is levelled, then a 30cm layer of silty clay soil is spread directly on top, followed by a thin layer (about 2cm) of manure which is lightly cultivated in, and finally the whole mix is topped off with a 10cm layer of sand. The tomato roots concentrate at the interface between the sand layer and the soil/manure mixture, and the sand acts as a mulch, reducing water evaporation from the surface. This gives a 'best of both worlds' situation: the relative ease of cropping in soil, and the use of a consistent growth media that can be replaced as necessary.

---

with soil from the vegetable patch works well (though don't use soil from an area where potatoes were grown recently, as they suffer similar ailments to tomatoes). As we now understand that most of the organisms responsible for soil sickness lurk in the top layer of the soil, digging out to the depth of a spade (about 30cm, or 1ft) is perfectly adequate. It's a good job for a cold winter's day.

'Plunging' Plants

This is a sort of hybrid planting method: it doesn't prevent soil sickness altogether, but rather, delays its build-up.

Start the tomatoes off in reasonably large pots of compost, then before they get too big to move, dig holes large enough to accommodate at least half the depth of the pot, and drop the pot in. Over the next few days water the pot as normal, but also run some water around the pot to help settle the soil. The plant roots will soon emerge through the drainage holes and start taking up water from the soil. (Enthusiasts for this method sometimes prepare the pots in advance by drilling a few additional holes around the side.)

Because most of the tomato root is contained in the pot and removed each year, the chances of disease carrying over between one crop and the next are reduced. Remember to give the pots a wash with a domestic bleach solution before using them again the following year.

This method can also be useful for outdoor crops if you have a particularly sunny spot in the garden where you like to grow tomatoes every year, or if the soil is of a clay texture and slow to warm up in the early season.

Using Grafted Plants

Plants grafted on to a disease-resistant rootstock cost considerably more than normal plants, but are a worthwhile precaution in some situations, particularly if the soil is something of an unknown quantity. Growing a single grafted plant alongside ungrafted plants will soon indicate the degree to which the ungrafted plants are being restricted.

Soil Biofumigation

Soil *fumigation* was extensively practised at one time, using an array of none-too-pleasant chemicals; *biofumigation* is a relatively new and completely different idea, safe to do, and is proving very effective in a number of situations. If the appropriate amount of time can be found, preferably in the early autumn, then this is worth a go.

It may involve terminating the tomato crop a couple of weeks earlier than usual to leave enough of the growing season for the biofumigant crop to reach a reasonable size, but as late fruit can easily be ripened off the plant, little or no yield is lost.

Biofumigation involves growing mustard, chopping up the plants very finely, then incorporating all the plant material into the soil quickly. As the plant material breaks down it releases chemicals (from the glucosinolate compounds that make mustards and some other brassicas hot) that have a suppressing effect on various soil-living pests, including a range of fungal diseases. Normally when this is done on a field scale, machinery is used to chop and incorporate the plant material into the soil, but in the small greenhouse a little improvisation is called for. The procedure is something like this:

• Order the mustard seed well in advance.
• De-leaf the tomato plants, cut the stems at soil level and remove them with all fruit attached; they can be hung up for the remaining fruit to ripen.
• Dig out the roots as completely as possible, clearing up every bit of tomato plant that can be found.
• Lightly cultivate the soil, water well and leave to drain. Broadcast the mustard seed on the surface and lightly rake it in.

The seedlings should emerge very rapidly, as the soil will still be warm. How large the mustard is left to grow is up to the individual; when this is done on a field scale the plants are left to get as large as possible, which means leaving them until the flowering stage, but it is unlikely there will be enough time to allow for this. Then comes the critical bit:

• Chop up the plants as finely as possible – go mad with the garden shears or electric hedge cutter, but do it quickly.
• Incorporate all the plant material into the soil – a small border fork is probably best for the job, as it doesn't need to go down too deep.
• Rake the surface level, and pat it down with the back of the rake.
• Throw some plastic sheeting over the top (old compost bags opened out are good) and hold the edges down with a few bricks. This seals in the fumes, which can then do their work.

If the greenhouse soil is not needed again until the spring, then it can be left like this all winter. If the soil is needed for, say, an early spring crop of lettuce before the next tomato crop, it should be left for three to four weeks, then given a light cultivation before planting.

6 CROPPING INDOORS AND OUT

WHEN TO PLANT TOMATOES

Whether cropping in a heated or unheated greenhouse or outdoors, the question 'When is the best time to plant?' usually means, 'How early can I plant and expect to get away with it?'

Gardeners have been pushing their luck on this question for many years; in its advice to war-time gardeners, the then Ministry of Agriculture in the UK sternly warns against planting outdoor tomatoes too early, stating 'It is foolish to hope that the danger of frost is past until at least the end of May'. Given the weather patterns over the last few years, this may seem excessively cautious, particularly when the garden centres are already carrying stocks of attractive-looking tomato plants in April – but whatever the current state of global warming, and whichever side of the Atlantic you are, the statement in the same document a few lines later is worth heeding: 'Little is gained and much may be lost by rushing plants out of doors a week or ten days before the weather has warmed up.'

However tempting the weather looks, and whether planting in a greenhouse or outside, a good guide to when it is all right to plant is to measure the soil temperature at rooting depth (about 10cm/4in). Tomato roots are notoriously temperature sensitive and do not appreciate less than 10°C, and are much happier at 14°C. If the soil or growth media is too cold, the tomato plant responds by not growing at all and showing a purple discoloration of the undersides of the younger leaves due to phosphate deficiency induced by the cold – phosphate is not being taken up due to the temperature being too low. Although the situation will right itself once the temperature warms up, the cold period gives the plant an unnecessary check.

EARLY PLANTINGS IN THE UNHEATED GREENHOUSE

Planting early in an unheated greenhouse avoids frost and makes the most of early growth. With soil-grown crops the following procedures should be observed:

Warm the ground before planting: It is possible to assist the soil-warming process early in the season – in the days when most greenhouse tomato crops were soil-grown, heating pipes normally propped up on bricks were lowered on to the soil surface to warm it up prior to planting.

If the greenhouse soil has not been disturbed from the previous season it should first of all be dug and broken down to aerate it; also if soil has been left over winter and is as dry as dust it will need a thorough watering, as bone-dry soil will not warm up effectively.

Polythene sheeting laid on the surface will help the ground absorb heat during the day; black polythene is favoured because of its heat-absorbing properties, but it is also particularly good at re-radiating the heat at night, especially under clear skies. Clear polythene, bubblewrap or horticultural fleece will warm the soil and also encourage the weeds to grow, which is perhaps no bad thing because they can then be hoed off before planting, giving the tomatoes a clean start.

Add some garden compost: Good quality compost made from plant material (particularly leaf mould) is often very dark, almost black in appearance. As well as digging compost into the soil, leave a thin layer on the surface or just lightly rake it in. This will darken the soil and help it absorb heat.

Check the temperature: Purpose-made metal-cased soil thermometers are available, but an easy way to check the soil temperature is to take a small bottle (something like a stubby beer bottle is ideal), fill it with water, and sink it up to its neck into the soil on the intended planting site; given a day or so to stabilize, the water will assume the temperature of the surrounding soil and can easily be checked with a conventional thermometer.

Maintaining the Temperature after Planting

Planting Through a Mulch

Laying some form of sheet material on the soil surface, cutting holes in it and planting through the holes gives several advantages:

- Water is conserved by stopping evaporation from the soil surface (in the greenhouse this helps a little in keeping humidity under control).
- The majority of weed growth is prevented.

- It stops disturbance of the soil surface when watering with a hose or can.

The most convenient material to use for this purpose is some sort of weave, either black 'ground matting', usually obtainable off the roll from garden centres, or the strong white material that the one tonne bags used by builders' merchants to deliver sand and aggregate are made of; these can usually be salvaged from a skip. Whether one is any better than the other as far as the plants are concerned is a moot point, as any benefit will only be found early in the season. The white surface reflects light back into the leaf canopy of the plant, but the black surface would keep the soil warmer.

Fleece Covers

As tomatoes need a minimum air temperature of 10°C for vegetative growth, don't expect the plants to get away particularly fast from early plantings. To try and keep the temperature up a little overnight and to give some protection against late frosts while the plants are small, fleece covering can be draped over them overnight.

'Passive' Solar Heating

Researchers in northern Greece and Turkey have come up with an ingenious method of storing a little of the sun's energy at minimal cost. Despite

An early planting in the greenhouse soil showing white mulch material, drip irrigation and 'passive solar heating' – there is room for a few more bottles.

plenty of sunshine, both countries suffer problems with early season plantings of tomatoes in their polytunnel greenhouses due to low night temperatures.

The technique that has been developed uses large (30cm/12in diameter) transparent plastic tubes filled with water – some have called them 'hot water bottles for plants'. These are laid on a layer of black polythene on the soil surface between the rows of plants, the aim being to cover somewhere between 30 and 40 per cent of the floor area with these water tubes. During the sunny daytime the water warms up, then at night this heat is re-radiated, keeping the air and soil temperatures over 1°C warmer than similar houses without tubes.

A way of improvising this technique is to use rows of water-filled 2ltr (3.5-pint) plastic soft drinks bottles or supermarket milk bottles placed on their sides nose to tail in the greenhouse, covering as much of the unplanted floor area as possible. Milk containers have a more angular profile so can be pushed together like paving blocks, whereas 2ltr soft drinks bottles may need wedging with bits of wood to keep them in place.

Do not expect fantastic results when trying this method in the UK: it should be realized that the temperature gain will not be as high as the researchers in Greece and Turkey experienced due to the smaller overall volume of water held by the bottles, and the fewer overall hours of sun in early season UK.

Remove the bottles once night temperatures improve, and use the space between the plants for companion planting or some salad greens or herbs to enjoy with the tomatoes.

A combination of techniques – soil mulches, water tubes and a fleece covering at night – gives a far greater advantage than individual techniques.

Establishing a Tomato Crop in an Unheated Structure

The suggested dates are relevant to the south of England; for northern England add twelve days, for Scotland add sixteen days.

Planting date: For an unheated greenhouse or polytunnel, planting can be risked from the first week in April, but it is a worthwhile precaution to have some fleece covers available, and some plastic bottles for passive solar heating.

Plant raising: At least six weeks' production time should be allowed; if raising the plants on the kitchen windowsill, go for a sowing date around Valentine's Day.

Greenhouse Preparation
- Wash the glass down on the inside to remove accumulated dust and dirt.
- With soil-grown plants, if no crop has been grown since the previous season's tomatoes, thoroughly soak the soil over a period of several days and allow to drain.
- Cultivate the soil deeply; tomato roots can go down nearly 1m (40in) given the chance, and the deeper the root system the less chance there will be of any problems with water stress later on.
- Incorporate composts/manures – traditionally a base dressing of fertilizers would be applied at this stage; although the plant will be slow to get away and will not need much nutrition in the first few weeks, it is worth incorporating a small amount of a high phosphate fertilizer, as due to low soil temperatures phosphate will be in short supply.
- Lay the fleece cover on the soil surface to assist in warming the soil – put a max/min thermometer underneath to give an idea of how things are doing.
- Clean the glass outside, particularly the roof – just a soft broom or car-washing brush and soapy water, then a rinse with clean water. Clean out the gutters and check the waterbutt.
- Hoe off any weeds that have emerged while the soil has been warming up, and check the temperature at about 10cm (4in) depth: a constant 10°C is needed.
- If using plastic mulch, install it and mark out the position of the plants.
- If using stakes as plant supports it is more convenient to put them in at this stage. Trying

to install a long wooden stake into a greenhouse border can be awkward as there is not much room to swing a hammer; an alternative is to use some short stakes at the early stage, then extend them before the plants get too tall by attaching sturdy bamboo canes held to the stake with a couple of Jubilee clips.

Plant it, Water it, Leave it

- Plants need to be spaced at about 45cm (18in) apart: dig the planting holes and drop the plants in – plant with the first truss facing the path.
- Give each plant a small individual watering to settle the soil around the roots, thereafter leave them alone for a week. The objective at this stage is to get the roots exploring the soil, and don't worry if there doesn't seem to be much foliage growth at this stage: this is due to low temperatures and light, not lack of water.
- Install as many 'hot water bottles' as you have been able to accumulate around and between the plants.
- Overnight put fleece covers over the plants – it's worthwhile to do this even if no frost is forecast as it keeps the temperature up a little overnight by stopping heat being re-radiated from the floor. This works best if the fleece doesn't touch the plant itself, so arrange it as a 'tent' effect. Try and get as many of the water bottles on the floor covered by the tent as well. It is important to remove the cover first thing in the morning, as the plants need all the light they can get at this stage.
- When some regular growth is observed, start watering the plants; they will not need much at this stage – every two to three days will probably suffice. Do not be tempted to liquid feed too early: it is important not to overdo the nitrogen, as promoting vegetative growth may cause abortion of flower trusses. With soil-grown crops it is safe to let the plants get to about 1m (40in) tall before starting liquid feeding.

Tomatoes Grown in Straw Bales

Developed in the 1960s, this is an interesting old technique and one of the first methods used in commercial production to bring tomatoes out of the soil (though in the long term the technique proved to be more popular for cucumbers than tomatoes). One of its advantages is that it can get round the cold root problem in the early season by generating some warmth of its own.

The basic idea involved setting out straw bales in rows, isolated from the soil by sheets of plastic, and soaking them over a period of several days with a strong solution of nitrogen fertilizers. This caused the straw to start to compost, resulting in it slumping, becoming a little more dense and increasing in water-holding capacity – and very conveniently the composting process generates heat.

The process was monitored by checking the temperature of the bales, and once the composting process started to slow down (indicated by the temperature starting to fall) the rows of bales were topped with a layer of potting compost into which the plants were placed. Rapid establishment and very vigorous vegetative growth followed as the plants made the most of the warm root environment and the nitrogen. At the end of

Purple coloration on the leaf undersides: this is indicative of phosphate deficiency brought about by low root temperatures, a common problem with early plantings.

the crop the straw would have largely decomposed and could easily be disposed of.

The technique went out of favour in the commercial world as it had a number of shortcomings. The amount of nitrogen released in the composting process was both unreliable and uncontrollable, which made growth difficult to manage, but the big risk which became more apparent as agricultural production intensified was that of damage from herbicide residues; tomatoes are notoriously sensitive to even tiny traces of the types of herbicides used on cereal crops, and there was always a high chance that some herbicide residue might remain in the straw.

Be Sure of your Straw

Assessed in retrospect, this method had quite a number of things in its favour; certainly to modern thinking on sustainability, the use of a waste product as a substrate, which at the end of the crop has decomposed to a useful garden compost, sounds like the way to go. However, those considering giving this technique a try should bear in mind they are taking something of a risk with the possibility of herbicide residues; ideally straw sourced from a grower of organic cereals should be used for safety.

OUTDOOR TOMATOES

Though outdoor crops cannot be planted as early in the season as greenhouse crops, in certain situations it is possible to gain an advantage and basically cheat. In the southern part of England in areas that are not obvious 'frost pockets' the incidence of killing frosts after late April occurs approximately one year in twenty, so in the South it is worth pushing your luck with some early plantings (say, the first week of May) if some form of natural shelter is available.

For plants in pots or growbags, any sheltered situation, particularly with a south or south-east facing wall or fence, can be exploited; plants against a wall gain much advantage from its physical shelter and a much warmer microclimate due to the wall absorbing heat during the day. Also any amount of roof overhang helps keep the

rain off the foliage, important in avoiding late blight.

With crops in a relatively open situation such as on an allotment, much can be done with the provision of temporary shelter early in the season. The emphasis here is on temporary, as later in the year it is better to have the plants open to airflow so that the foliage dries quickly from dew or rainfall. Once again, late blight is the problem.

With outdoor crops grown in the soil, the soil temperature should again be the deciding factor on how early it is worth taking a risk on planting.

A row of plants, whether determinate or indeterminate types, can be sheltered for the first few weeks of their life with a low tunnel structure clad with either fleece or clear polythene sheeting. (Given a choice, fleece is the better option for tomatoes as it allows air exchange and stops conditions underneath from becoming too humid.) If this is the intention, then the site can be prepared and the structure erected several weeks early to help warm the soil. As the plants grow larger the cover can be removed, or if the condition of the cover is past its best, simply cut down the centre of it to allow the plants to push through.

LOW TUNNEL STRUCTURES

Low tunnel structures took over from the old glass 'barn' or 'Chase' cloches as ways of advancing the growth and maturity of plants. Various types are available, usually as kits containing hoops and a cover. If shopping around, look for the types that have the tallest hoops as these are the most suitable for tomatoes.

For those who enjoy improvising, these structures are easy to make; the supporting hoops are usually made of wire, but long whippy hazel branches or lengths of alkathene water pipe will make taller, stronger hoops. Covering materials can be polythene film or fleece, usually available from larger garden centres, cut to length from a roll.

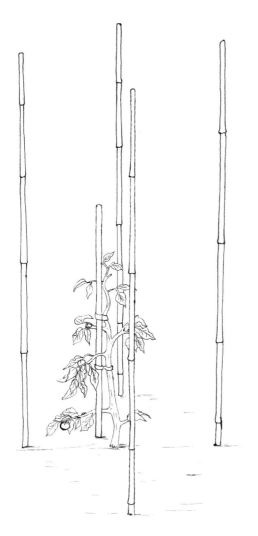

Protection for individual plants outdoors using a clear plastic rubbish bag with the base removed.

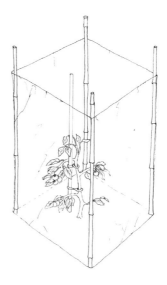

For individual plants, individual shelters can be made by arranging four canes around the plant, forming the corners of a square. Using these it is possible to 'wall the plant in' on all sides, the main effect of which is to reduce wind speed, so the plant stays slightly warmer as a result. The quickest way of doing this is to use either a clear plastic rubbish bag with the base opened out (if this is not done, rainwater will gather in a puddle on the top and weigh it down), or a netting bag such as is used to pack brassicas and onions; either can just be slipped over the canes and pulled down to ground level. Other possibilities are short lengths of bubblewrap or fleece, which need to be arranged around the canes and then joined by stapling.

ESTABLISHING TOMATOES IN CONTAINERS

Growbags

Emerging in the early 1970s, the forerunner of what we recognize as a 'growbag' – sometimes

Making a double growbag.

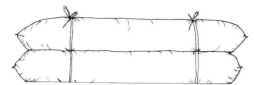

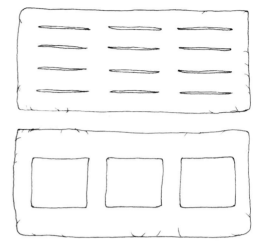

also called 'peat module' or 'bolster' – was initially used for commercial tomato production. These were developed and became very popular in Guernsey where greenhouse soils had grown tomatoes for so many years that disease problems were particularly bad.

The compost-filled 'Grobag' (spelled thus without the letter 'w') first appeared on the market in 1973 by courtesy of the Fisons company; the Grobag was a minor revolution for the home production of a number of crops, especially tomatoes, although it did take a bit of getting used to.

Some gardeners have mixed results with tomatoes in growbags, particularly later in the season when the need for water and feed is high. Like all plants growing with a restricted root volume, careful management is needed. On hot days a tall tomato plant carrying fruit will easily use 1.5ltr (about 3 pints) of water per day, so assuming three plants per growbag, an average water requirement of about 5ltr (over a gallon) per bag per day in midsummer is to be expected. It should be remembered that growbags originally came from commercial tomato production where automated drip irrigation is routinely used, and they work best with this type of system.

Peat or Alternative?

In recent years a range of bags containing peat-free or peat alternative media has appeared alongside the standard peat-based bags. Which do tomatoes prefer? Both types can give equally good or poor results, and success is largely down to management, tomato plants being tolerant of a wide range of growth media.

Preparing and Planting Growbags

Before planting, always prepare the bag by dropping it on its edges a few times – though not from too high or it is likely to burst – as the compost in the bag will have become compacted while standing on a pallet in the garden centre, and this loosens it up. When this has been done, pat the surface of the bag level and make sure the compost is evenly distributed along its length.

If using indeterminate plants, use three plants per standard bag as maximum; in many cases with the bigger, more vigorous F1 hybrids two is better and more manageable. With bush or determinate types, three plants is fine. Most standard growbags are 30ltr compost capacity, which if planted with three strong-growing indeterminate tomatoes can be difficult to manage through high summer, particularly if hand watering. There is a range of larger growbags of some 50ltr capacity, which hold a lot more water, and are a good idea if time only allows watering once a day. Unfortunately they seem to be more expensive on a 'per litre of compost' basis than the standard bags.

An alternative idea is to make a double growbag of 60ltr capacity: obtain two standard 30ltr-sized bags, cut out three sections of plastic in the top of one, place the other alongside it upside down, and slit the plastic in inch wide strips in the areas corresponding to the cut-outs. Quickly flip the second bag over on top of the first, and no

Planting on a growbag, rather than in it: the plant retains its pot, and roots spread via the drainage holes.

compost should be lost. A couple of strings around both bags will hold them together until the plants root through from the top to the bottom bag, by which time they will be well and truly joined together.

There seem to be two schools of thought regarding the planting of tomatoes into growbags: the first is to use small plants, take them out of their pots, create some holes in the growbag and drop the plants in so the whole compost ball is buried. The second is to plant on it, as opposed to in it. Initially grow the tomato plants in larger-than-usual pots – say, 14cm (5.5in) rather than 9cm (3.5in) – stand these on top of the bags and cut circles out of the plastic using the pot as a guide, then just press the pots into the compost to a depth of 3cm (1in) or so, making sure all the drainage holes are covered. The plants then root out into the bag via the drainage holes in the pot.

If prepared properly, the second method can make hand watering easier, as the water can be applied to the tops of the pots.

Plant Support

Ideally plants in growbags are best supported from above, using strings attached to a suitably solid overhead support. Failing this, canes can be used, but the bags are not deep enough to offer support, in which case frames are available into which the growbag and three supporting canes will fit. If the bag is placed on a soil surface then bamboo canes can be pushed through the base of the bag and into the ground for support, but beware of doing this if the reason for using grow-bags is because the soil is suspect, as the plants may take the opportunity to root through into the soil.

A home-made support can be easily constructed from a scrap wooden pallet: cut the pallet in half, screw short wooden stakes to the strengthening blocks in the corners and centre, then attach canes to these with Jubilee clips or wire.

Pots

Pots are perhaps the most versatile container for tomato plants; they can be ornamental as well as functional, they allow a choice of compost, and watering/feeding is usually easier than with grow-bags. The choice of container and the type of compost used is entirely up to the grower, and only limited by budget.

Terracotta pots always look good, and give the added benefit of stability when the plants get tall. Remember that unglazed terracotta pots lose water from the porous clay, so will need more frequent attention than glazed pots or plastic pots of a similar size.

Plastic pots containing a peat-based compost can become unstable with tall plants, and will need some extra securing late in the season. If the site is at all breezy, then consider putting a 50mm (2in) layer of gravel in the bottom of the pot to add some weight, and/or use a John Innes potting compost (which is considerably heavier than the

Growbag stands made from pallets sawn in half with canes attached.

peat-based mixes but more expensive), or possibly a 50:50 mix of John Innes and a peat-based compost.

It is possible to do a combination planting in a large pot, with an indeterminate plant in the centre supported by a cane, and two to three small determinate plants around the edge; alternatively include some basil and/or *Tagetes* for companion planting.

When planting a tomato into a pot, it can be useful to take advantage of the extra depth offered and place the plant deeper, so that a few inches of stem are buried – tomatoes easily produce roots anywhere along the stem, and this will give the plant an improved root system.

Some sort of mulch or covering for the top of the pot is useful – if watering with a can the surface of the pot is constantly disturbed, so the plant roots never get to occupy the full volume of compost.

Hanging Baskets

There are many miniature cultivars which are intended for container production, particularly in a hanging basket, and they are ornamental as well as functional – but just one word of warning: even the miniature cultivars can be surprisingly heavy with a full load of fruit, so make sure the supporting bracket is up to the job.

Traditional moss-lined wire hanging baskets

LEFT: **If a mulch is used on top of pots it stops the top layer of compost being disturbed when watering with a hose or can, so allowing the plant to root into the entire volume of compost.**

BELOW: **Bush tomato 'Whippersnapper' in a hanging basket.**

RIGHT: **Styrofoam box used for packing broccoli.**

BELOW: **Preparing the box with a layer of gravel.**

always look good, but lose water from all surfaces – it is better not to overload them with plants, or watering will become a three-times-a-day chore. To help with the watering problem, consider one of the newer compost products, which contain water-retaining agents. Alternatively 'Swell gel' can be added to a standard compost. This re-markable – though unfortunately quite expensive – material absorbs something like 200 times its own weight in water, and needs to be thoroughly mixed in at the time the basket is planted.

Ring Culture Revisited

The technique of ring culture was developed for greenhouse crops, though it can be adapted for outdoors. It involved raising plants in compost using bottomless pots (or rings), which were then stood on a bed of some sort of aggregate – washed and weathered ash and clinker from a coke fire being a popular medium at the time. This medium was contained in a shallow trough, often just a simple wooden frame lined with a sheet of polythene.

The idea was that the bed of aggregate was kept well watered and the compost 'rings' received an occasional dose of liquid feed. This encouraged the development of two different root systems by the plant, the feeding roots that stayed in the compost, and the large water-absorbing roots that explored the aggregate. A big advantage to this system is that the bed of aggregate can hold a good reserve of water, so the plants do not go through the wetting/drying cycles associated with other forms of container growing. This is obviously useful for irregular watering; however, there is an opinion that ring-cultured tomatoes lack the intensity of taste that can be achieved by other methods because the plants are grown in a wet as opposed to a dry regime.

It is quite a cheap technique to adopt: little is used in the way of compost, and the aggregate can be recycled year to year providing it is given a thorough hosing down at the end of the season to remove bits of tomato root, then preferably left outside overwinter to let the rain and frost get to it. There are many variations on the basic technique – boiler ash and clinker are not as common as they once were, but plenty of other aggregates can be used successfully – pea gravel and 10mm gravel, or a mixture of gravel and coarse grit works well and is inexpensive.

A Gravel Box

The gravel box is a variation on the ring culture idea, and uses the type of lidded Styrofoam boxes that are used to pack broccoli in ice, and can be scrounged from street markets. It can be employed in two ways: either long term for production along the lines of the ring culture method, or short term to plunge pots to decrease the frequency of watering needed (while the owner is on holiday, for example). The boxes do not take up appreciably more room than pots, and are nicely self-contained.

Make a row of drainage holes through the side of the box 50mm (2in) or so from the base, and put in a layer of 10mm-sized gravel (available in 25kg bags from a builder's merchant: one bag is plenty for two to three boxes) up to the level of the drainage holes. Put the box in its final posi-

---

ROCKWOOL

Introduced to the UK in the early 1970s, this material soon became the most popular substrate for tomato production, a position it still occupies to this day. Rockwool (or 'stonewool' to the Dutch) is made from a type of basalt rock, which is heated to melting point (around 600°C) and spun into fibres, which are then made into an array of slabs, blocks and cubes. In appearance it looks similar to loft insulation material. Because it is specifically manufactured for the job, rockwool can be made to a specific density to give ideal water-/air-holding characteristics for a healthy root system, and as all plants experience the same root environment, crop uniformity is improved.

---

tion before adding the gravel, as it will be heavy and awkward to move afterwards.

Cut the lid to accommodate the size of pot used (it is sometimes easier to cut the lid in half first of all, then trim to the shape of the pot), and make a second small hole in the lid to allow for watering.

Plunge the pot into the gravel, making sure the drainage holes are covered, arrange the lid, and then water the gravel until water comes out of the drainage holes.

It will take a few days for the plant to establish and start sending out roots into the gravel, then it can be managed as a ring culture plant, receiving liquid feed in the pot at intervals, and the gravel topped up with water as needed.

Tomatoes in Hydroponics

Hydroponic production (sometimes also known as soil-less culture) describes a technique whereby all the mineral nutrition the plant needs (all the major, minor and trace nutrients) arrive dissolved

Hydroponic feed solutions are usually provided as a two-part concentrate, only combined in a diluted state.

in the irrigation water, and the medium in which the plant grows plays no part in the nutrition process. This allowed for cheap, chemically inert materials such as sand and gravel to be used to grow the plants in, and with no need for soil, crops could be grown in many new areas provided water was available.

The idea behind hydroponic production is not particularly new, with pioneering work dating back to 1929, but practical commercial applications of it were not immediately forthcoming. The first commercial hydroponic systems emerged in the late 1940s, but even these did not immediately catch on, because compared to other methods hydroponic crop production is more complex to undertake and demands more careful management.

Applications of hydroponic techniques are many and varied; in the commercial world most tomatoes are grown in small volumes of an inert mineral medium known as a substrate, rockwool being the most popular, with the hydroponic feed being delivered down small drip tubes. For the amateur grower the scope of hydroponics is very wide indeed and encourages those who enjoy experimenting, as many other types of media can be used successfully.

Why Do It?

In general terms, hydroponic growing methods have a lot going for them. Obviously there is no need for soil, so there is very little restriction to where systems can be set up, plants can be grown in very limited spaces, and it's very economical on inputs in that very little gets wasted; but the main reason that amateur growers adopt hydroponic systems is that they find them interesting.

Some who grow by hydroponics enjoy the technical side of the process and like to experiment, building their own systems and mixing their own feeds, but for those who don't, there are many 'hobby' hydroponic systems now available as self-contained kits which do a great job of fitting plants into the minimum amount of space. Similarly, ready-mixed feed concentrates formulated to either hard or soft water are readily available, which simplifies one of the more exacting and technical aspects of the process.

The drawbacks are that it takes a while to get used to working with a hydroponic system, there is obviously a financial outlay for the equipment and an electricity supply is needed, also the neighbours will usually assume you are growing cannabis; however, once these are all resolved, a fully planted 'hydroponicum' is a fascinating thing.

Propagating Plants for Hydroponic Systems

For best results, plants intended for hydroponic systems should be propagated in a similar medium to which they will be grown, as plants grown conventionally in pots of compost often have difficulty adapting to an inert growth media. The favoured media for producing young plants are vermiculite and small cubes or plugs of rock-wool. Horticultural vermiculite (don't use the grade that is sold for insulation purposes) is usually used as a covering for seed trays after sowing, but it can be used in place of compost to fill small pots for plant raising.

If growing tomatoes in this way, it often helps to germinate the seeds first of all (on a few folds of kitchen towel), then transfer them carefully to pots of vermiculite or rockwool plugs just as the root is starting to emerge.

The main difference between using these media and propagation in compost is that the young plants will need very dilute liquid feed right from the start, as there are no nutrients in the vermiculite or rockwool. Before the seeds are transferred, the media will require soaking in the nutrient solution.

Tomato seedlings propagated in rockwool.

7 PLANT TRAINING AND ROUTINE OPERATIONS

THE ANATOMY OF THE TOMATO PLANT

The indeterminate type: The plant will produce on average seven to eight true leaves before producing a flower truss; thereafter it will produce two more leaves before the next flower truss, and so on. In each leaf axil a sideshoot will be produced; the shoot produced in the leaf axil below a truss is called the 'truss shoot' and is more vigorous than the other sideshoots. How tall the plant eventually gets depends on the individual cultivar, the length of the internode space (the distance between the leaves), and the amount of general vigour, which varies considerably between cultivars.

The usual method of growing this type of plant is to support it either by tying the stem to a vertical cane, or twisting it round a string (sometimes referred to as cordon training), restricting the plant to a single stem by regular removal of sideshoots. Later when the fruit starts to ripen the lower leaves are removed to allow better exposure of the ripening fruit to light.

The determinate or bush type: A multi-stemmed plant, which theoretically needs no support but in practice often does, if only to keep the fruit off the ground as the stems can break down under the weight of the fruit. Unlike the indeterminate types, no regular sideshoot removal is needed, but as the fruit starts to ripen the plants may benefit from a trim to thin out the non-productive growth and allow better air circulation and light penetration.

Intermediate or semi-determinate types: Cultivars described as intermediate or semi-determinate (essentially tall-growing bush varieties) will definitely require support.

TRAINING INDETERMINATE TYPES

In a greenhouse, plants can be supported either by stakes or canes, or by strings secured overhead

OPPOSITE: **Vine-ripe tomatoes.**

RIGHT: **Truss development on the determinate plant.**

A semi-determinate or intermediate type requires several sticks for support.

them; this saves any possible root damage. If using strings, a useful trick is to dig the planting hole, make a couple of loops in the end of the string, drop this in the hole and position the plant on top of it: after a couple of weeks the roots will have firmly anchored it in place.

Tying Plants to Canes

- It is important not to put any undue pressure on the stem: leave room for it to increase in girth.
- Ties go above trusses not below; in this way the weight of the truss is better supported.
- Don't be too enthusiastic to secure the very top of the plant: the growth here is brittle, and it is surprisingly easy to snap out the growing point.

Training Plants up Strings

- Twist the string round the plant, not vice versa.

Substantial supports are needed for indeterminate types grown conventionally as single-stemmed plants.

to the framework of the greenhouse, or to an overhead wire which itself is secured to the gable ends. If using the latter method, be aware of the extra load the plants are putting on the structure of the greenhouse: it is not unknown for a greenhouse to be brought down by the weight of tomato plants loaded with fruit.

For outdoor situations, make sure the stakes or canes used are sufficiently sturdy; even a single tomato plant carrying three or four trusses of fruit is surprisingly heavy, and a bout of bad weather such as a late summer thunderstorm can bring the whole lot crashing down unless the supports are set firmly in the ground.

If using stakes or canes it is best to push these into the ground first of all, and then plant against

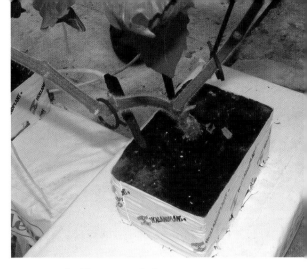

A mature, double-stemmed plant on a commercial nursery.

- The string completes a circuit of the stem every two leaves.
- The string goes behind or above a truss, never below it.

Variations on Training

There is no need to be conventional and grow indeterminate plants as a single vertical stem – granted it's the easiest method, but it's not the only one.

Training for Two Heads

Rather than remove all sideshoots and restrict the tomato to a single stem, it is possible to allow one or more sideshoots to grow to form extra 'heads', giving a two- or even a three-stemmed plant. This is a good way of getting more yield from a limited area. Commercial growers often set out a single row of plants, then let them produce two 'heads', which are then trained to the left and right, giving two rows of cropping stems from a single row of plants. A two-headed plant can be achieved in two ways:

- Firstly, remove the growing point altogether above the two cotyledons when the plant is very small. Two sideshoots of equal size and vigour will then grow.
- Alternatively and perhaps a better method, or useful if plants are bought rather than propagated at home, let the plant establish as normal, but curb all enthusiasm to remove sideshoots. When the first fruit truss appears, retain the sideshoot that appears in the leaf axil directly below it (the truss shoot), let this

ABOVE: **Developing a double-stemmed plant from the propagation stage – remove the top growth as shown, just above the cotyledons.**

BELOW: **Development of new shoots following the removal of the top of the plant.**

ABOVE: **Development of a double-stemmed plant.**

TOP LEFT: **An ideal truss shoot to train as a second stem.**

MIDDLE LEFT: **Allowing the first truss shoot on the plant to develop.**

BELOW LEFT: **Developing the second stem: train the truss shoot away from the stem at a wide angle; this allows the stem to thicken and form a strong junction.**

BELOW: **Double-stemmed plant in midsummer.**

establish until it is long enough to tie into a second supporting cane or string, and in a short time it will grow as a second stem. If growing plants in containers this method works quite nicely with small cherry-fruited types, which tend to have small leaves and widely spaced internodes.

Be aware that there is an additional risk that a two-headed plant becomes dangerously top heavy late in the season, and some extra support may be required.

Training for Two Bottom Trusses

A technique that was adopted by commercial growers in the 1930s and 1940s was to retain the first truss shoot as if starting to grow a two-headed plant, but only letting it grow until it had produced a fruit truss, then stopping it. This essentially produces a plant with two bottom trusses, and nearly doubles the amount of early fruit on the plant, with the extra truss ripening at about the same time as the second truss on the main stem.

This technique was developed in an era before mass imports, and as early season home-grown tomatoes had a good price premium, the extra effort involved was worthwhile; however, it is no longer used commercially.

In practice the method works quite well on tomatoes in pots, and is well worth a try. A short cane is needed to support the new shoot, otherwise it breaks down under the weight of the fruit. Better results are obtained in letting the sideshoot grow one or two leaves beyond the truss before stopping it.

Training for Horizontal and Upside-down Plants

Provided it is remembered that the plant will always try to return to the vertical so extra training will be required to keep it in any other state,

Ripening fruit on the extra truss; this plant had lost the first truss completely and sustained some damage to the second.

the training of indeterminate tomato plants is only limited by imagination.

Horizontal plants: Training a tomato along a balcony handrail or similar, with the fruit trusses hanging over the side like bunches of grapes, works well, though it is important not to be too enthusiastic with the training: the growing point of the plant will always be attempting to return to the vertical, so it is best to leave the top 45cm (18in) or so of stem to its own devices and just tie in the lower parts of the stem as the plant grows. The top part of the plant can be very brittle, and there is a considerable risk of breaking the top off the plant completely if trying to pull it down to the horizontal.

A plant can also be trained along a horizontal wire close to the ground, the object being to put the entire plant under cloches or a low plastic tunnel for protection. This is sometimes done with soil-grown outdoor crops late in the season to help ripen the late fruit – initially the plant is grown vertically supported by a stake in the 'conventional' manner, then the plant is untied from the stake, the stake laid down supported by a couple of forked sticks about 30–45cm (12–18in) from the ground, and the plant reattached. The whole assembly is then covered with cloches, a low polytunnel, or a layer of 'fleece' to protect it.

Upside-down plants: An 'upside-down' plant can be grown in a hanging basket or raised container, with the stems trailing over the sides. If

Using a low plastic or fleece tunnel to ripen late fruit on outdoor plants.

trying this with a hanging basket, go for a small cherry-fruited cultivar and use a two-headed plant with the stems trained opposite each other, or the basket will look very unbalanced. Beware that a hanging basket holds less reserves of water than most other containers, and watering can become a frequent job – but the result can look quite impressive.

TRAINING DETERMINATE TYPES AND 'INTERMEDIATES'

Determinate or 'bush' tomatoes theoretically do not need training or support, however if left alone the stems of many varieties get pulled down to the ground under the weight of developing fruit, and a lot of potentially good fruit is spoiled because it is sitting on the ground and attracts slugs. One way around this is to put a good layer of straw under the plants, as might be done with strawberries; this keeps the fruit off the soil.

Individual stems on these plants can be tied to canes, but as each plant produces several stems the job can get somewhat tedious if a lot of plants are involved. Several plants, or an entire row of bush tomatoes can be supported on horizontal canes or wires attached to short stakes – if a double row is used and the plants positioned in the middle, the stems are just draped over the wire or cane to each side.

Intermediate types will definitely need the stems supporting; one way is to start with a single support cane as if it were an indeterminate plant, then as other stems appear add extra canes pushed into the ground at angles so the plant resembles a fan-trained fruit tree. Alternatively the type of cage supports as used for herbaceous plants can be used, but they can push the stems close together, giving restricted air movement.

POLLINATION AND FRUIT SETTING

Tomatoes are self-fertile: that is to say, they do not need to be cross-pollinated (receive pollen from another plant) in order to set fruit. Looking at the tomato flower in detail, the yellow centre comprises a cone of pollen-bearing anthers, in the centre of which is the stigma; this means that the pollen does not have very far to go, so pollination should be foolproof. Unfortunately this is not entirely so, and commercial growers have always had a problem with early season glasshouse crops in getting fruit to set: due to low light levels, the style (the little stalk on which the stigma sits) elongates, pushing the stigma beyond the end of the anther cone. With outdoor crops, pollination can be adversely affected by bad weather and cold

Support for bush or determinate plants using horizontal canes.

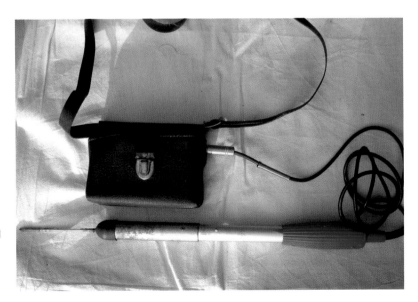

The battery-powered 'electric bee' used to shake the flower trusses and get the pollen moving.

A hive of bumble bees for pollination; it is only since most pesticide use was stopped in favour of biological pest control that this has been possible, as bees are very sensitive to a variety of pesticides.

conditions, as pollinating insects are prevented from flying.

Pollination involves two processes – the transfer of pollen from the anther to the stigma, followed by the successful germination of the pollen grain.

The transfer of pollen: This process happens best in warm, dry conditions, and for many years this was manually assisted by growers, by agitating the flower trusses to get the pollen moving; this operation involved rattling the supporting strings or stakes with a stick, or using a device called an 'electric bee' to vibrate the flower trusses and shake the pollen off in clouds. (Some keen amateur growers improvise to excellent effect with an electric toothbrush.)

These days as most commercial growers produce crops with little or no pesticide treatment, it has been possible to install hives of bumble bees in greenhouses to do the job of pollination, a big saving in time for the growers.

The germination of the pollen grain: To assist in the second process, conditions of high humidity are beneficial to the development of the pollen grain. In greenhouses this can be achieved by 'damping down': spraying water on the path, then leaving the ventilators and door firmly shut for an hour or so.

Truss pruning 'Gardener's Delight'.

OTHER ROUTINE OPERATIONS

The following operations may start sounding like hard work, but none of them takes very long to do, and once a week is usually enough.

Truss pruning

This involves removing some of the flowers or young fruit from a truss, so limiting the amount of fruit, and may be done for several reasons. With large beefsteak types the sheer weight of fruit can break the truss away from the stem, so for safety they are better restricted to two to three fruits per truss. Cherry types with long fruit trusses can suffer from under-sized, poorly developed fruit at the very ends of the truss. Those growing fruit for showing may reduce the number to get fewer fruit of a more even size and shape.

Truss pruning can be done either by removing some of the flowers on the truss, or by waiting to see how successful pollination has been before deciding how many to snip away. Pruning is easily achieved with sharp kitchen scissors.

Leaf Removal

When the fruits start to ripen, the lower leaves of the plant can be removed up to the next ripening

ABOVE: **Results of truss pruning – improved development of the later fruit.**

RIGHT: **Truss pruned.**

A plant featuring a 'split leader'.

RIGHT: **Decide which head to remove, then cut through the stem avoiding the flower truss.**

BELOW: **Job done.**

TOP: **Compare the size and vigour of the truss shoot with that of the sideshoot in the leaf axil below it.**

MIDDLE: **Snapping out a sideshoot: twist it one side to the other and it will break away.**

BOTTOM: **The sideshoot breaks off cleanly.**

truss – it is considered that by this stage any leaves below a ripening fruit truss are not contributing much to the plant, and removing them allows for better light penetration and air circulation. This should be done by breaking them off rather than cutting: support the stem with one hand, tweak the leaf up, then down, and it should snap away cleanly – this leaves a wound that heals more quickly than a cut so there is less chance of fungal infection.

Before disposing of any leaves removed, turn them over and examine them: the older leaves often support the greatest population of 'biological control' predator and parasitic insects (even if these have not been introduced, there are plenty of wild species that will become established from mid- to late summer). If the leaves have any unhatched aphid mummies or Encarsia scales, leave them around the base of the plants for a few days to give them a chance to hatch.

Sideshoot Removal

Remember that of all the routine operations carried out on tomato plants, sideshoot removal should be done as the last job.

Working upwards, remove the sideshoots by carefully tweaking them from side to side: they should snap out cleanly. Towards the top of the plant it is best to leave the small, undeveloped sideshoots until the next time – more damage may be caused by trying to remove a tiny sideshoot than its presence justifies.

The 'Split Leader'

Sometimes a plant will appear to divide into two

growing points of equal size and vigour just after producing a truss; this is nothing to be concerned about, but if a single-stemmed plant is all that is required, then one of the 'heads' will need removing. This is one of the few times a knife is used in tomato trimming operations; decide which 'head' to remove, then cut through the stem trying not to get too close to the truss.

Fruit Harvesting

Basically harvest tomatoes as you need them, but in cases of glut it is best not to leave the ripe fruit on the plant for too long as removing fruit takes some load off the plant and maintains steady vegetative growth. It is important to remove all fruit when ripe even if the fruit is undersized or damaged; anything left on the plant to get over-ripe stands a good chance of attracting fungal disease.

Harvest by holding the ripe fruit in the palm of the hand (do not grip with fingers) and press with the thumbnail against the 'knuckle' joint just above the calyx.

Vine-ripe types should be harvested by snipping away the whole truss close to the stem with sharp secateurs.

If possible avoid harvesting for a couple of hours after watering, if the fruit is disturbed while the plant is actively taking up water it sometimes splits straightaway.

END OF SEASON OPERATIONS

Stopping Plants

With greenhouse-grown plants, stopping may need to take place when the plants have run out of available room and are threatening the roof.

It is sometimes recommended for outdoor crops in the UK that the plant is allowed to produce four or five trusses, then stopped to encourage the fruit to ripen.

Although this is not a hard and fast rule, and in some years it is possible to ripen more trusses than this, there seems little point in letting the plant produce much in the way of vegetative

---

FRUIT SPLITTING

In late summer it is often found that an increasing amount of fruit splits as it ripens, though some cultivars seem worse affected than others. This can be due to a combination of a number of factors, but is often caused by low night temperatures combined with irregular waterings. Not much can be done regarding the temperatures, but changing waterings from evenings to mornings may help. Other than this, start harvesting the fruit a bit under-ripe and allow it to ripen fully on a windowsill.

---

growth in late August/September, as any further fruit that is developed will not stand any chance of ripening.

Having decided when to stop the plant, decide which is the last fruiting truss to be kept, let the plant produce a further two leaves, then snap out the top of the plant. Treating the plant in this way doesn't stop vegetative growth completely (which can cause all growth to stand still), but gives the plant a shock.

The plant will attempt further vegetative growth by producing sideshoots from the axils of the uppermost leaves. If the weather is still relatively warm it is best to manage this growth by leaving a couple of the uppermost sideshoots in place, letting them grow to produce two to three leaves, then removing the growing points; in this way the vegetative growth is severely curtailed, but the plant is still kept in an active growing condition and the fruit will continue to develop.

End of the Year Harvest

There comes a time each year when the tomato crop has to come to an end – the actual date can be extremely variable, depending on late summer/early autumn weather conditions, and the incidence of certain diseases, particularly late

ABOVE: **Cherry tomato 'Ruby' grown as a double-stemmed plant – each stem was stopped after nine trusses had been produced.**

BELOW: **The good, the bad and the ugly: all tomatoes that could be salvaged from the end-of-season harvest of an outdoor crop.**

blight – but a decision needs to be made as to when the last fruit ought to be salvaged while it is still possible to do so. Tomatoes harvested on the truss, whether vine-ripe or not, can last a surprising length of time if stored properly (it is not unusual to harvest in late October and still have tomatoes available at Christmas), and although they may not be very appealing for fresh consumption, they are fine in pasta sauces and the like.

It is important only to try and store healthy-looking fruit that is undamaged. Whole trusses of fruit last well if hung up in a cool, dry atmosphere – hanging the trusses from hooks or stringing them at intervals along a line works well; fluctuating temperatures and a damp atmosphere are the enemies.

An old gardening book recommends that individual tomatoes are stored in shallow wooden trays in a single layer with the fruits not touching each other, and covered with a sheet of paper. Similar storage conditions can be created at no expense by scrounging some shallow cardboard

fruit trays from a supermarket. Trays that previously held kiwi fruit or figs are particularly good, even better if they retain the cardboard liner which separates the individual fruits.

Ripening Under-Developed Fruit

Tomatoes harvested green can be ripened successfully if they have reached something like their final size. Under-developed fruit will store well enough, but will remain green, and should be used up in green tomato recipes.

There are a number of tried and tested tomato-ripening methods – perhaps the best known is to put the fruit in a lidded cardboard box with a ripe banana for a few days. Many ripening fruits release a gas called ethylene, the presence of which accelerates the ripening process, and bananas are particularly good at it. Working in this way, it is possible to ripen stored green tomatoes more or less as needed.

Alternatives to Storing Fruit

Too many tomatoes, not enough room: when left with a glut of ripe and semi-ripe fruit at the end of the season, they can be treated in a number of ways as an alternative to storing them.

Tomatoes do not freeze well as fruits, but cooking the surplus to a pulp with a little olive oil, then passing this through a sieve to remove the skins, gives a type of passata, which freezes very well.

A type of dried tomato can be made by halving the fruit, then covering it with a 50:50 mixture of salt and caster sugar, which serves to draw out much of the water. After twenty-four hours or so, brush the mixture off and put the halved fruits in a barely warm oven to dry slowly. The fruit can then be bagged and frozen.

Using up imperfect and damaged fruit that would not store – add garlic, onion, peppers and olive oil and make it into pasta sauce (30min in the oven and a few seconds in the food processor).

8 IRRIGATION AND FERTILIZATION

NUTRIENTS AND FERTILIZERS

Like their close relatives potatoes, tomatoes are often described as 'gross feeders': vigorous growing plants that need comparatively large amounts of nutrient to maintain them in good fruiting condition through the season. The usual approach to tomato nutrition takes two forms: first, an application of nutrients is given to the soil or growth medium prior to planting – this is called the *base dressing*, to get the plants established and to encourage initial vegetative growth.

Once the plants are established and the first fruit is starting to swell, some extra nutrition is needed. Formerly this was given as *top dressing*, involving periodic small applications of fertilizer to the surface of the soil or growth medium and watering them in; however, this practice has been largely replaced by *liquid feeding*, where fertilizers are dissolved in the irrigation water.

A third method sometimes employed to correct a nutrient deficiency in the plant is *foliar feeding*. This entails a particular nutrient being applied to the whole plant in solution as a fine spray, so it is absorbed by the foliage.

Mineral Nutrients

What the plant needs to extract from the soil or growth medium is a range of mineral nutrients; these are classified as major, minor and trace nutrients according to the overall amount that plants use.

Major nutrients: Sometimes called macro nutrients, these consist of three chemical elements – nitrogen, phosphorus and potassium, usually collectively known as NPK (the K standing for kalium, the old apothecary name for potassium).

Minor nutrients: Sometimes called the secondary macro nutrients, these are needed in less quantity than the majors. This group consists of the elements magnesium, calcium and sulphur.

Trace elements or micro-nutrients: This final group is needed by the plant in miniscule quantities, though their absence usually causes a disaster. They are iron, copper, zinc, boron, chlorine, manganese and molybdenum.

'Straight' fertilizers are those that supply one (or sometimes two) of the major nutrients, examples being sulphate of ammonia (nitrogen), single superphosphate (phosphorus) and potassium nitrate (potassium and nitrogen in a 3:1 ratio). These types of fertilizer are not always stocked at garden centres and may involve a certain amount of shopping around to obtain.

Most fertilizers sold today, whether in liquid or solid form, are referred to as 'compound' fertilizers; these contain the three major nutrients in differing amounts, and possibly some of the minor and trace nutrients, depending on whether they are intended as general purpose fertilizers or are formulated to the needs of a particular crop. The straight fertilizers pre-date the compound types, and it was largely the necessity of blending several straight fertilizers together in order to provide a balanced diet for crops that caused the compounds to be developed.

Thanks to legislation going back to the

Fertilizers and Feedstuffs Act in the late 1800s, anything sold as a fertilizer has to have its content in terms of percentage plant nutrients prominently displayed, and the major nutrients always listed in the order NPK. When reading the label on a pack of tomato fertilizer, however, it appears that there is more to this than initially meets the eye. Thus the element nitrogen is frequently provided in three forms: nitrate, urea or ammonia. Depending on the fertilizer, it may contain nitrogen in just one or all three of these forms, in which case the label will give a percentage figure for total nitrogen, plus an additional breakdown of the components.

The content of the element phosphorus is expressed in terms of phosphorus pentoxide soluble in water; potassium content is expressed in the form of potassium oxide. If included, the minor and trace nutrients are usually listed just using their chemical symbol. The major nutrients are also expressed in ratio form, which allows easy comparisons between different fertilizer brands. For example, the old allotment favourite National Growmore (introduced as part of the 'Dig for Victory' campaign, and still going strong) is a general purpose compound fertilizer containing 7 per cent N, 7 per cent P and 7 per cent K. This is also known as a 1:1:1, describing the ratio of nutrients to each other.

The requirement for mineral nutrients differs according to both the plant and the plant's stage of development. Back in the 1920s it was shown that in one season a greenhouse-grown tomato crop extracted four and a half times the amount of nitrogen from the soil than phosphate, and a massive nine times the amount of potassium.

Before concluding that the ideal tomato fertilizer should contain nutrients in these ratios, it should be noted that much of the nitrogen is needed in the initial vegetative growth stage, whereas most of the potassium is used when the plants are bearing heavy loads of fruit. This gives a case for using two different fertilizer combinations, one higher in nitrogen for the early stages of the crop, followed by one higher in potassium for the main fruiting season.

Controlled Release Fertilizers

Controlled release fertilizers are specialist types of compound fertilizer consisting of a soluble compound fertilizer of NPK, plus a range of trace elements manufactured into round pellets, with the pellets covered in a specialized coating which is micro-porous, allowing water to enter and dissolved nutrients to slowly leach out. Such is the technology that these products are manufactured to release their nutrient over a certain time

Standard information on a bag of fertilizer: the percentage of each plant nutrient, and the figures expressed as a ratio.

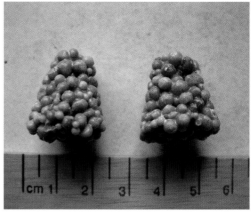

Plugs of controlled release fertilizer. These are excellent in containers and hanging baskets – just push one into the compost.

period, so three-, six- and twelve-month timed release versions can be found.

These are very useful products for growing plants in containers.

As well as in pelleted form these products are available in a type of plug, which saves having to mix the granules into the compost at potting time – just push a plug into the container next to the plant.

Unique features of these products are that they do not overdose the plant in the early stages of growth, and little nutrient is wasted by being washed out of the medium, even with the most enthusiastic watering or the wettest weather. The only down side is that they can be expensive.

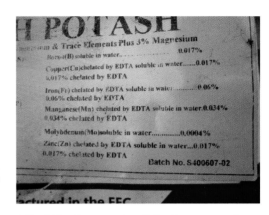

A liquid feed preparation listing its content of chelated trace elements.

'Organic' Fertilizers

There can be some confusion as to the meaning of this term: an organic fertilizer is one of organic origin, based on animal byproducts such as pelleted poultry manure, bone meal, or hoof and horn, or plant-based products such as seaweed extract. In addition to this there are a few mineral fertilizers of 'natural' origin, such as ground rock phosphate, which are approved for use in commercial certified organic production systems, so these have also picked up the 'organic' tag.

Organic fertilizers release their plant nutrient content over a period of time as the material has to be broken down by the action of soil-living bacteria; however, different materials break down at different rates, and the breakdown process is strongly influenced by temperature and soil moisture, so the release of plant nutrients is not reliably slow and steady. This can lead to occasional over-availability, particularly of nitrogen.

Chelated or Sequestered Trace Elements

With some compound fertilizers the trace elements may be listed as 'chelated' or 'chelated by EDTA'. Ignoring the actual chemistry involved, the process of chelating involves combining the trace element with an organic acid, in which form it is largely unaffected by pH

levels so the chance of trace element deficiency induced by pH level is much diminished.

Liquid Feeds

Liquid feeds tend to be the mainstay of the home tomato grower. They are supplied as soluble crystals or as a liquid concentrate, and are usually dosed into a watering can. Some gardeners prefer to feed their plants once or twice a week with a more concentrated feed, others to feed at every watering with a more dilute solution. Whichever is chosen, it is important to keep to the instructions on the packet/bottle regarding dilution rate.

If liquid feeding regularly, it is a worthwhile precaution to stop every ten days or so and just give the plants plain water for a couple of days. Plants do not take up all nutrients evenly, and this helps to wash out any excess that may be starting to build up in the soil or compost.

Home-made Feeds

Many keen growers have their own special or preferred recipes, particularly when it comes to liquid feeds. The old technique of steeping a hessian sack of manure in a full water butt still has its enthusiasts; the liquid feed made by such a method will have a low nutrient value, so can be used at every watering without risk of overdosing. Feeds of this sort will be highly bacterially active, which is thought to be beneficial for the root environment; however, take care not to splash any on to ripening fruit.

Comfrey Extract

Comfrey extract is made by decomposing a pile of fresh comfrey leaves (the wild comfrey *Symphytum officinale* or the Russian comfrey *Symphytum X uplandicum*) in a plastic container with a tap at the base. The decomposition yields a thick black liquid, which is periodically drawn off and diluted (one part extract to about twenty parts water) before being used. It is popular as a summer liquid feed, being very high in potassium. A particular drawback of this material is its smell, which takes some getting used to at the best of times and gets a great deal worse in the heat of high summer. Manufacturing opportunities may be limited if your neighbours have sensitive noses.

Comfrey leaves can be gathered from the wild, but many prefer to establish their own plants in a shady corner. The selection of Russian comfrey known as Bocking 14 developed by the legendary Lawrence D. Hills is the one to go for: it has sterile flowers (so it doesn't seed itself everywhere) and must be propagated vegetatively by root cuttings. Cuttings are usually available in the autumn from organic gardening specialists. Alternatively there are now preparations available consisting of dried comfrey foliage compressed into pellets, but the extract still smells!

Nettle Tea

Nettle tea is another useful if smelly concoction, but very easy to make. Its manufacture simply involves steeping the tops of fresh stinging nettles in water for a few weeks, stirring occasionally, then straining off the extract and diluting it (about one part of extract to ten of water) before using. Enthusiasts for this material say that the perennial nettle (*Urtica dioica*) contains its maximum content of minerals when just coming up to flowering, so should be harvested at this stage for the most nutrient-rich tea.

FEEDING SOIL-GROWN CROPS

The Influence of pH

pH level is something that is quite often overlooked with soil-grown crops. Tomatoes do not appear to be particularly pH sensitive, but if the soil has been producing crops for a few years and the previous season's crop was unsatisfactory and showing signs of nutrient deficiencies, it is well worth checking the pH level of the soil. The overall soil acidity or alkalinity has an influence on the availability of plant nutrients, in particular the trace elements, which often have a very narrow operating 'window', becoming unavailable above or below specific pH levels.

If the ground is regularly cropped the element calcium (a minor nutrient) will get used up over time, leading to the soil becoming increasingly acidic. The level usually recommended for tomatoes is between 6.0 and 6.5, which is just slightly acidic; however, on most mineral soils tomatoes seem to be tolerant of pH levels from 5.5 to 7.0.

As pH is very easy to check (various test kits are readily available), there is no reason to let the situation get to the point where too much corrective action is needed. If soil acidity is dropping much below 6.0, fertilizers containing calcium – such as calcified seaweed, or some straightforward garden lime (calcium carbonate or calcium hydroxide) – incorporated into the soil will soon correct it. Ground dolomite limestone is worth seeking out as an alternative to garden lime – this is a mixture of calcium and magnesium carbonates, which does the same job of correcting over-acidity but also supplies the nutrient magnesium as a bonus. Excessively high pH levels (above 7.5) are unlikely unless on a calcareous soil; should this situation occur it is not so easy to deal with, as there is no quick way of acidifying the soil.

Adding Composts and Manures

Back in the days when all greenhouse tomato crops were soil grown, it was usual practice to incorporate a fairly heavy dressing of manure, and then add a base dressing of fertilizer prior to planting. In the early 1900s tomato growers in the Lea Valley routinely used about forty tons of horse manure and one ton of compound fertilizer per acre prior to planting. It did not take long for research to show that this was overdoing it somewhat, but high populations of plants in a greenhouse environment do need high levels of nutrition.

Incorporating manure into the soil for a tomato crop is still considered worthwhile, the main advantage being improved water retention in the rooting zone rather than nutritional benefit; however, one present-day problem with manures – which the growers of the early 1900s would not have faced – is the possibility of herbicide residues. Cereal straw used as bedding for animals could still contain traces of herbicides used in the cereal crop, the smallest amounts of which can badly affect tomato plants. As a precaution the old gardeners' recommendation of 'well rotted manure' should be strictly adhered to – the older and better rotted the manure, the more chance that any herbicide residues will have broken down.

Spent mushroom compost is sometimes available as a bagged product; it is recommended for its high nutrient value, but it is also highly alkaline, so for any sites with soil pH approaching 7.0 it should be treated with some caution. Garden compost is about the safest material to use; it should be free of contaminants (unless grass clippings from lawns treated with selective weedkillers have been included) and tends to have a relatively high potassium content.

Stem and foliage distortion indicative of herbicide damage; these plants were contaminated by a spray being used outside the greenhouse.

Adding Other Fertilizers

The subject of base dressings is always difficult, as the amount of nutrition available in the soil will depend heavily on the soil type, and how the soil has been treated in the previous season. Commercial growers would opt for a soil analysis to assess the nutrient availability, and calculate how much more to add; a gardener could also take this option. Soil analysis laboratories charge according to how detailed an analysis is needed (major nutrients only, or a full analysis), and will advise on procedures for soil sampling. Alternatively there are soil-test kits widely available, which enable analysis for the major nutrients.

A third option is to make an educated guess, which is not too difficult if the history of the site is known.

With regard to tomatoes and their need for the major nutrients, the one difficult area is likely to be phosphorus; this element is not usually deficient, but with early plantings the uptake is reduced due to low temperatures, so it is a worthwhile precaution to make sure some is available. Two possibilities to safeguard against lack of phosphorus are:

- Apply a fertilizer containing phosphate only – use the straight fertilizer Triple Superphosphate in the region of 70–100g/m^2 lightly forked in.

- Apply a general compound fertilizer; many potato fertilizers are useful as a base dressing for soil-grown tomatoes as they tend to be formulated with reasonably high P and K levels, but use light applications only (up to 100g/m^2), as high levels of potassium can induce magnesium deficiency.

On balance there are probably more difficulties caused by overdoing a fertilizer base dressing than by being cautious and under-dosing. Modern liquid feeds are very good, and as greenhouse plants need routine watering it is easy enough to apply some feed if plants are seen to be not growing as well as expected.

Soil-grown Crops Outdoors

The information in the section above would also apply to outdoor crops, though there is a case for even smaller quantities to be used. Outdoor plants need to develop a sturdier root system than protected crops, particularly if summer waterings are likely to be irregular. By using only small amounts of nutrients and incorporating them well into the soil the roots are encouraged to explore a wider area.

PLANTS GROWN IN CONTAINERS

Composts, particularly peat-based composts, do not hold on to nutrients to the same degree as soil, so using a heavy base dressing gives no advantages. Generally speaking, plants grown in compost will need some supplementary nutrition at an earlier stage of growth than plants in the soil.

Many gardeners like to make their own mixtures of growth media for planting containers, blending ingredients such as peat, bark or coir with compost made from garden waste, leaf mould and so on. If doing this, remember that the nutrient content of these composts is likely to be very variable, as will the pH, so there can be no

hard and fast recommendation for how much additional fertilizer to put in as a base dressing. With home-made mixtures it is quite easy to overdo the nitrogen, which pushes the plants into very lush and rapid vegetative growth, often at the expense of the early fruit. As a precaution if using garden compost, either don't add any extra nitrogen fertilizers to the mix, use a controlled release fertilizer, or forget the base dressing altogether and be prepared to start liquid feeding earlier than usual.

Growbags

All growbags contain a base dressing, enough to get the plants started, but as three plants in a 30ltr bag is a very heavy load, they will need liquid feed from the appearance of fruit on the first truss. 50ltr bags or double bags will support the plants for longer before extra feeding is needed.

IDENTIFYING SYMPTOMS OF NUTRIENT IMBALANCE

Some nutrients have classic symptoms of over- and under-supply, whereas others are harder to spot; the main ones are identified below.

Nitrogen

Nitrogen is the most common nutrient to show both deficiency and excess, but conveniently both conditions are easy to correct.

If the plant is very dark green and producing large, lush foliage, then it has too much soluble nitrate at its disposal. Plants find nitrogen impossible to ignore, and if it is available they take it up, leading to a condition called 'luxury absorption'. In this condition of strong vegetative growth fruiting is inhibited and the plant is very prone to pests and diseases. Excess nitrogen doesn't usually occur unless someone has been very heavy handed with fertilizer or manure applications, but as the nitrogen content of animal manures and garden composts can be notoriously variable, it is quite possible to over-supply without realizing.

The condition is quite easy to rectify – nitrates are very soluble, so over-watering the plant helps to wash out the excess nitrates, but eventually the plant will use up the excess and return to normal growth.

Nitrogen deficiency shows as the foliage losing colour and becoming increasingly yellow in appearance; growth is slow and new foliage is reduced in size, with older leaves starting to die off. This often shows in plants in pots that are just coming up to the transplanting stage, having exhausted the feed available and becoming pot-bound.

Phosphorus

Both phosphate deficiency and excess are uncommon, particularly in soil-grown crops; however, in compost-grown crops either is a possibility.

Phosphate is associated with root growth, and obviously restricted root growth means restricted shoot growth, so a plant looking stunted and un-willing to get on with growing when conditions are good may be experiencing a lack of phosphate. Another clue may be the appearance of the foliage, in that the leaves appear to have a slight purple tinge on the undersides and at the edges.

Phosphate deficiency can be induced by low temperatures in the soil or compost, so is fairly common in early plantings. Not much can be done about this, and it usually sorts itself out as soon as conditions warm up.

Potassium

Tomatoes have a very high demand for potassium, particularly when fruiting, so it is a key component of all liquid feeds used during the fruiting period. As a general rule feeds used once the plants start fruiting should contain potassium and nitrogen in the ratio of two to one, plus magnesium. Potassium deficiency shows as a marginal leaf scorch and mottling of the older leaves, whereas excess shows as hard, stunted foliar growth with a blue tinge. The usual cause of things going wrong is the potassium and nitrogen levels being out of balance.

Magnesium

Magnesium deficiency is about the most commonly occurring nutrient deficiency seen on mature tomato plants – the lower leaves start to go yellow, leaving just the veins showing green. (Nitrogen deficiency also causes leaf yellowing, but the whole plant has a slightly yellow, unhealthy appearance.) If the plant is short of magnesium it removes it from the lower older leaves and translocates it to the new growth, so the deficiency always shows at the base of the plant and gradually works its way upwards if not corrected.

Because the uptake of potassium and magnesium are linked, high levels of readily available potassium can reduce magnesium uptake to the point that deficiency results; the other possible cause is related to pH, as magnesium becomes less available under alkaline conditions.

Luckily a magnesium deficiency is quite easy to rectify: for a 'quick fix' obtain some Epsom salts (magnesium sulphate) from the chemists, dissolve 10g in 1ltr of water, and spray on the foliage, concentrating on the lower leaves, in the early evening; usually one or two applications does the job. Thereafter change the liquid feed for a brand with a higher magnesium content, and all should be well.

Iron

Iron deficiency sometimes occurs if pH levels are above or around seven, and for this reason the deficiency is sometimes called lime-induced chlorosis. The symptoms are very similar to that of magnesium deficiency (though it does not occur anything like as commonly), the difference being that they first show at the top of the plant on the new growth, and if not corrected the growing point can be lost.

The easiest way of dealing with iron shortage is to obtain a feed containing chelated or sequestered iron, or chelated trace elements. If used as a liquid feed the chelated compounds are largely impervious to the effects of pH, and the plant can take them up regardless.

Blossom end rot, or BER.

Calcium

Tomatoes are often spoilt by a disorder named blossom end rot, where the base of the fruit shows a large black patch of dead tissue. This is associated with calcium shortage, in that insufficient calcium has reached the developing fruit to allow all the cells to form properly. In most cases the calcium isn't in short supply in the growth medium, but it doesn't get to where it is needed due to a combination of environmental factors upsetting transport within the plant. The fault is usually due to irregular watering, so suspect this first before getting too worried about calcium content, as actual calcium shortage is quite rare. The pH level is the first and most obvious clue.

WATERING AND WATERING SYSTEMS

Tap, Rain or Grey?

Although many gardeners prefer to use rainwater where possible, most will find themselves using tapwater for much of the time, particularly through the height of summer, usually because of limited storage capacity for rainwater. Having said this, it is worthwhile installing water catchment where possible: firstly it's free, and secondly the 'quality' of rainwater can in many cases be considered better, as it contains little in the way of the dissolved salts responsible for 'hard' water.

PLANT RESCUE

There can be instances when despite the world's best preparation everything goes horribly wrong, and the plant starts to look very unhappy indeed, whether through nutrient imbalance, a fungal disease or some other form of root damage.

A rescue attempt can be made on an indeterminate plant by encouraging it to produce adventitious roots from higher up the stem. Remove the lower leaves, construct a circular 'collar' out of cardboard about 15cm (6in) deep and wide enough to drop over the top of the plant. Place it around the stem at the base and fill it with a good quality, general purpose potting compost; then water, and cross your fingers. Hopefully in about five days the plant will start pushing out adventitious roots from the area of the stem buried in the compost, and start drawing water and nutrition from there.

This method can also be tried if the stem gets damaged at the base from cutworm activity, or to boost plants that don't manage to produce an extensive root system and start to 'flag' in the middle of hot summer days.

Generally speaking, if using either tapwater or rainwater there ought to be no quality problems, but be careful with rainwater collected immediately after a dry spell, as the rain will have washed off a mixture of pollutants from the roof surfaces. Keep water butts lidded; excluding the light will limit the growth of algae. A lid also stops mosquitoes breeding in the water, prevents accidents to unsteady birds attempting to get a drink, and of course limits water loss by evaporation.

Grey Water

This is defined as water that has served once for domestic duties such as bathing or washing up.

Much has been researched on the uses of grey water for irrigation purposes, most of it in countries where hot summers give routine restrictions to the use of water to irrigate the domestic garden.

Most research appears to agree that grey water can be used for irrigation, but not universally; for instance, if a house has a water softener plumbed in, then grey water should not be used. Domestic water softeners use sodium (obtained from salt) to chemically displace the calcium in hard water, and high sodium levels interfere with potassium uptake in plants. Tomatoes in particular cannot tolerate sodium to any excess.

Grey water from domestic laundry is also suspect due to the possibility of increased chlorine content (due to bleaching agents in detergents).

If using grey water it is advisable to restrict its use to soil-grown crops, and to alternate applications with tap- or rainwater from time to time. Grey water collected in buckets for future use should not be left in a warm environment such as a greenhouse due to its possible bacterial content.

Automatic Watering Systems

Before installing any automatic irrigation system that connects directly to the domestic water supply it is important to check the state of the plumbing; currently any 'outside tap' installation must by law incorporate a non-return mechanism to stop the possibility of any water going back into the system, but older installations may not have this. The easiest way to update an old system is to do a direct swap with a new outside tap that incorporates a non-return valve.

For many years commercial tomato growers have been using irrigation systems that send water to individual plants via a network of small-bore pipes, calibrated so that each plant receives the same amount of water. This type of irrigation is known generically as drip irrigation. More recently small versions of this system suitable for the amateur grower have become more available; the most common types involve a small battery-operated timer and valve, which usually fix directly on to a tap.

Using a manifold on an outside tap will allow an automatic watering system to be attached semi-permanently while still leaving the capacity to use a hosepipe.

These little timers are programmed in two ways: the number of applications or 'starts' in a twenty-four-hour period (usually between one and four), and the amount of time the water will be applied for at each start (1–5min). Many also have a manual override to allow extra applications on particularly hot days. Apart from being very useful for when you go on holiday, these allow the adoption of a little-and-often watering system, which is ideal for plants in a restricted

volume of media such as growbags, and prevents the wet/dry cycle caused by only watering once a day.

Setting the system up is easy enough: use a good quality battery in the timer and it will last all season, route the small-bore pipes out of the way behind the containers, and position the drippers where they can be seen. It is usual to

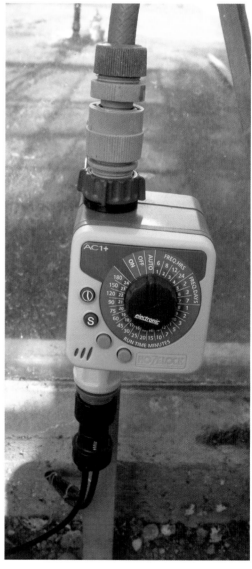

The timer – one outlet pipe has been temporarily blanked off, as the full capacity was not needed.

allow one dripper nozzle per plant, which is all right if all plants are in the same size of container, but if working with a mixture of container sizes some juggling might be needed – two or three drippers in large pots, single drippers in smaller ones.

Once set up, it is worthwhile experimenting with the system to get a suitable combination of watering cycles. The instructions may give the average output of the nozzles (in terms of litres per hour), but this will be influenced by water pressure. To check, run the system for ten minutes and collect the output from a few drip nozzles in individual containers. Measure the results, and multiply by six to get the output per nozzle per hour.

When the plants are establishing they will only need one or perhaps two waterings daily, largely depending on the size of the container and the volume of compost each plant has available to it. Once fruiting starts, a 'little and often' watering regime is preferred as the best tasting tomatoes are grown fairly dry, and wetting/drying cycles often lead to fruit splitting. Set the timer to give the maximum number of applications, but fairly short watering cycles.

There are other types of automated system. One recommended for greenhouses uses a type of thermostatic valve rather than a battery-operated timer, and the flow of water is increased as the temperature rises. Others are independent of battery power or mains water supply, and rely on gravity to deliver the water from a tank placed at a suitable height.

The dripper, the business end of the watering system, should be placed where it can be seen easily.

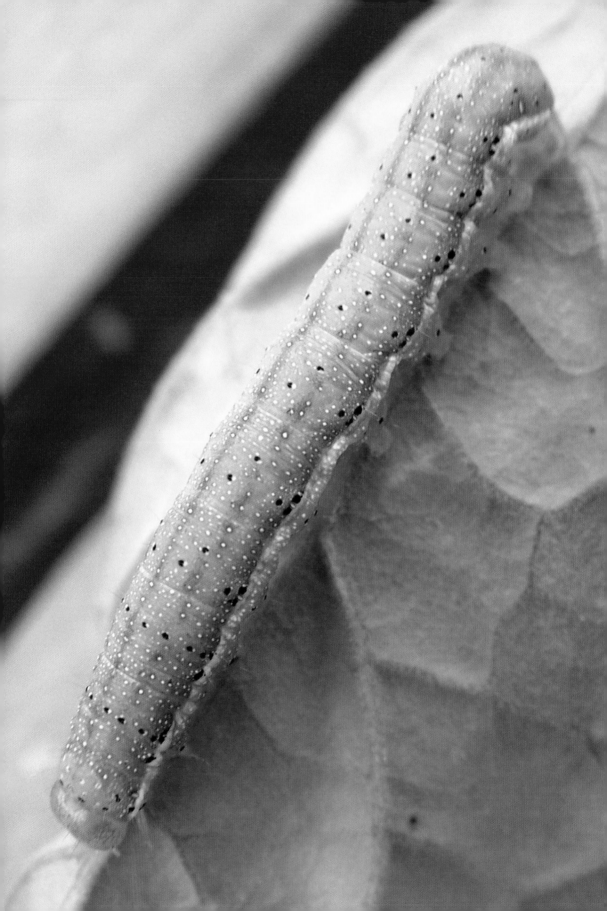

9 PESTS, DISEASES AND DISORDERS

Lists of pests and diseases always seem to make depressing reading, but a distinction needs to be made between what *could* happen, and what actually *does* happen most of the time. Although there are many conditions that tomato plants can fall victim to, some are fairly specific to certain growing conditions (for example, may be fairly common under glass, but rarely show up outdoors); some diseases rely heavily on a certain combination of environmental conditions to occur; and insect pests are around in high populations in some years and barely noticeable in others.

Tomatoes can have inbuilt resistance or tolerance to quite a range of diseases (particularly fungi) and some pests, or can be given this resistance by grafting on to a suitable rootstock.

Where resistance is present, a system of letter and number codes has evolved to indicate the level of resistance or tolerance in any particular cultivar. Each disease is identified by a letter, and in the case of fungal diseases where more than one strain of the fungus is known, each particular strain is identified by a number. For instance the popular F1 hybrid 'Shirley' is listed as TMC5F2, which means it has resistance to the following:

- TM – tomato mosaic virus
- C5 – all five races of the fungus *Cladosporium fulvum*, or tomato leaf mould
- F2 – strain 2 of *Fusarium oxysporum lycopersici*, a soil-borne fungal disease

The list below shows the main code letters used:

OPPOSITE: **Caterpillar of the tomato moth, also available in green.**

- A – *Altenaria*, a soil-borne fungal disease
- V – *Verticillium wilt*, another soil-borne fungus
- F – *Fusarium oxysporum lycopersici*, a soil-borne fungus; as fungi often exist in different races or strains, so resistance to one strain does not mean resistance to all. This indicates a particular strain, named strain 0
- F2 – as above, but a different strain
- P – *Pyrenochaeta lycopersici*, another fungus, responsible for corky root disease
- N – *Meloidogyne species*, nematodes or eelworms that cause root galls
- M – *Phytophthora infestans*, otherwise known as late blight or potato blight
- C – *Cladosporium fulvium*, the fungus responsible for tomato leaf mould. This also exists in separate races identified as 1–5, so the letter may have a number attached
- T or TM – tomato mosaic virus (sometimes referred to as tobacco mosaic virus)

FUNGAL DISEASES

As always, prevention is far better than cure, and a few simple precautions are always worthwhile – such as clearing away debris from the previous season, and disinfecting pots and canes before re-use. In recent years the number of pesticides available to the gardener has diminished considerably, so curative treatments are not always available.

With soil-borne fungal diseases that persist from one year to the next there are two main approaches: either use resistant cultivars or plants grafted on to resistant rootstocks, or forget the soil and grow in isolated media (pots or bags).

Verticillium and *Fusarium*

These two fungi are sometimes known as 'vascular wilts'; they are soil living, and when they infect the plant they clog up the vascular tissue (xylem and phloem vessels) which the plant uses to transport water and foodstuffs. When attacked by either fungus the plant foliage gradually wilts, starting with the older leaves and working steadily up the plant. Eventually the plant dies, as water can no longer be moved up the stem.

The presence of *Verticillium* can be confirmed by cutting a transverse section of the stem, which will show a dark discoloration or staining, sometimes pinkish-looking, in a ring just beneath the skin. Symptoms of *Fusarium* appear very much the same, though sometimes accompanied by the presence of yellow stripes on the stem.

These diseases were far more common when all tomatoes were soil grown, as they can persist year upon year, and also as they are soil living they can romp through a whole crop. For the amateur grower, these diseases are more likely to show up in a greenhouse where the soil has been used for tomato crops for several years, than in any other situation. If this happens, consider growing plants in bags or pots the following year, or using grafted plants.

As a precautionary measure, watering the plants with compost tea may give some protection against these and other soil-borne fungal diseases. Compost tea is rich in a whole variety of micro-organisms including fungi, and there is a school of thought that the presence of non-pathogenic fungi on and around plant roots makes life more difficult for pathogenic fungi trying to infect.

Corky Root Rot

One of the most common soil-borne diseases of tomato, corky root rot can survive in the soil for a number of years. Symptoms show as a wilting of the plant, but the pattern is different from that exhibited by *Verticillium* or *Fusarium* in that it starts with the top and gradually works down. The plant may appear to recover overnight as there is less stress on the damaged root system, but eventually the wilting becomes more serious and the plant will die.

Remove affected plants and dig out as much of the root as possible; the fungus can be identified as large corky patches on the thicker roots.

Cladosporium (Tomato Leaf Mould)

This fungal disorder affects the leaves; in the main it appears on greenhouse crops and is less common on outdoor crops as the spores need conditions of very high humidity (90 per cent plus) combined with high temperatures in order to germinate. The fungus causes leaf spotting on the undersides of the foliage. The spots turn light brown or grey as spores are produced.

At the first signs of this, or any other fungal disorder, remove infected leaves and drop them straight into a plastic bag, then tie up the bag securely and bin it. If caught early enough and the infected material is removed, it usually isn't fatal.

Grey Mould

Caused by the fungus *Botrytis cinerea*, grey mould is an opportunist sort of disease that affects many plants. It usually occurs on dead or dying plant tissue first of all, then can spread to living tissue if conditions are favourable – like many fungi, it prefers high humidity and a damp environment, so is far more prevalent in greenhouses than outdoors. The main problem it causes with tomatoes is when it infects the stem, where it causes dark patches or lesions, which may appear slightly sunken. If these spread around the stem effectively girdling it, this can kill the plant.

Take off any dead or dying foliage and clear it up, and increase air circulation around the plants by removing a few leaves. If stem lesions occur, a method that is said to prevent the fungus spreading is to paint the lesions with vinegar.

Didymella Stem Rot

This rot is also sometimes called canker, and is

caused by the fungus *Didymella lycopersici*. Like botrytis, it causes lesions on the stem, but can also infect the fruit trusses, damaging the calyxes and causing the fruit to drop. It is mainly a disease of greenhouse crops, where it survives from year to year on bits of plant debris. Spores of the fungus are easily spread by water splash, so take care if watering with a hosepipe and keep the water away from the stems.

Plants can survive a low infection of this fungus, but it is important to avoid further spread. Plants with lesions at the base of the stem are best removed, which calls for some careful handling to avoid dislodging and spreading spores.

The start of an infection of *Phytophthora infestans*, or late blight. As soon as leaf damage like this starts to show, salvage all available fruit.

Late Blight

Caused by the fungus *Phytophthora infestans*, this is the same fungus responsible for potato blight and is the fungal disease that is most prevalent on outdoor tomato crops.

One of the signature features of late blight is the fast rate at which it becomes established and romps through a crop; moreover once it is established there is little that can be done to eradicate it.

This fungus needs certain temperature and humidity levels over a period of time to become established, and by close monitoring of the weather conditions it is possible to forecast when blight is likely to occur. Potato growers use this information to time fungicide applications.

Because the foliage needs to be wet for the fungal spores to germinate, tomatoes grown outdoors in open ground are the most likely to be affected. Those grown in pots or bags up against a house wall where the roof overhang keeps much of the rain off, will often escape as the leaves remain drier. Plants in greenhouses or polytunnels are also at risk – although the foliage remains dry, the humidity levels are much greater inside the structure than outside, particularly if it is shut up overnight following a warm day.

When blight damage is noticed on the foliage, urgent action is required: cut off all parts of damaged foliage, place them in a plastic bag, seal

The beginning of the end – late blight spreading to stems and fruit.

the top and bin or burn it – do not put it on the compost heap, and afterwards wash the knife or secateurs in disinfectant. Inspect the plants every day, and repeat the process on affected plants. Once the lesions of the fungus appear on the stems the end is not far away, so rescue what fruit remains undamaged by cutting away the trusses and bring it indoors to ripen.

Make sure all blighted plants are destroyed, and all debris picked up. Pots and canes used for the plants can be given a bath in a domestic disinfectant before re-use.

There are now some cultivars available that have a partial resistance to blight.

Blighted fruit – do not put this on the compost heap.

Nematodes

Should soil-grown tomato plants display the wilting symptoms typical of some of the fungal diseases mentioned above, there is a possibility that the roots are being damaged by a completely different pest: nematodes, or eelworms. There are two species of importance: the root knot eelworm which only infects tomatoes, and the potato cyst eelworm, which, as its name implies, also infects potatoes, and is the reason that tomatoes should not be planted in ground that has recently held potatoes.

As with the fungal vascular wilts, there is not a great deal that can be done, and the approaches are to use a resistant cultivar or a grafted plant on a resistant rootstock, and/or to avoid the soil and grow in pots or bags.

Tomato Mosaic Virus

Tomato mosaic virus (TMV) displays a variety of symptoms, frequently showing on mature plants as a pale green or yellowish leaf mottling effect, often accompanied by distortion or curling of the leaves. It is not always fatal, but fruit size and number are both reduced, and growth can be stunted. It is important to remember that many of the more modern cultivars are resistant to this virus, and any paling or yellowing of the foliage is more than likely to be a trace element deficiency.

TMV is caused by the tobacco mosaic virus, and historically growers have often banned smoking in tomato houses in the belief that this virus can be passed on by those who smoke a pipe or hand roll tobacco and then handle plants.

If the virus does show (and it is fairly uncommon) there is nothing to be done as a curative measure, but it is important to make sure it is not spread to other healthy plants. Virus-infected plants should be removed and destroyed.

PLANT DISORDERS

Greenback

Greenback is a condition where the 'shoulders' of the fruit remain green while the rest ripens; when the fruit is cut open the green portion shows as a very tough lump of flesh. It was once the bane of growers' lives, as greenbacked fruit was either not marketable or fetched a much lower price.

The disorder appears to be genetic, in that some cultivars are prone to it and others are not; however, by a steady process of development nearly all varieties introduced since the early 1960s are greenback free, so only those growers cultivating older 'heritage' varieties are likely to come across it. If growing a greenback-susceptible variety there is not much that can be done to stop the disorder showing up, though it has been noted that the condition appears worse if the plant starts running low on potassium.

Blossom End Rot

This condition can easily ruin an otherwise perfectly good truss of tomatoes, and is particularly annoying on cherry-fruited types (a small patch of BER on a large fruit can be cut out, but cherry fruits are usually too damaged to salvage – though having said this, these types appear to be less susceptible to the condition). BER is caused by a calcium deficiency in the developing fruit: where insufficient calcium has been available to completely develop the cell walls, an area of dead tissue results.

Fruit affected by BER.

Aborted flowers, the result of two very hot days.

This calcium shortage is often caused not by a shortage in the feed, though tomatoes do have a reasonably high calcium requirement, but by the calcium not getting to where it is needed, usually due to water stress. The disorder generally results when the plants have been under a particularly heavy load – for instance, three mature plants in a standard-sized growbag on a hot afternoon.

Try to avoid wetting/drying cycles in the growth medium, and keep greenhouses well ventilated, as high humidity levels can make the condition worse.

Aborted Flowers

An entire truss may fail to form, or it may partially form, or it may sometimes fully form but the flowers die off and drop before opening. An isolated incidence of this occurrence is probably just bad luck; if early in the season it can be caused by a few hours of unseasonal bright sun following a dull spell, or high temperatures that cause the plant a high level of water stress. If occurring later in the season, inspect the damaged area for evidence of fungal spores.

INSECT PESTS

The presence of a few insect pests is no cause for undue panic. Compared to many vegetables, tomatoes don't seem to suffer too badly from insect pests, and as most of these are leaf or sap feeders leaving the fruit unaffected, perfectly good tomatoes can be produced on a very rough and damaged-looking plant. The key to effective insect pest control is regular monitoring to make sure the population doesn't get out of hand.

Tomato Moth

As far as UK growers are concerned, this is about the only caterpillar of note to affect tomatoes badly. As with many butterflies and moths, the population of the tomato moth has good years and bad: in some years it doesn't show up at all, in others it can be around in mid- to late summer.

Damage shows as chewed foliage, and if the plants are inspected closely (try in the mid-afternoon, as the caterpillars appear to be most active around this time), the caterpillars are quite large and easy to see – they vary in coloration between shades of green and brown. As the plants will usually be in fruit by the time the caterpillars appear, any form of chemical spray is inappropriate; although there is a 'safe' compound available for caterpillar control, based on the bacterium *Bacillus thuringiensis*, it is unlikely to be justified on the sort of scale that most gardeners work. The easiest solution is to pick the caterpillars off (wearing gloves or using kitchen tongs if necessary). Inspecting the plants daily and picking off the caterpillars when seen will soon have the damage under control.

Cutworms and Wireworms

These cause occasional damage on bush tomatoes grown outdoors. Cutworms are the larvae of the yellow underwing moth, wireworms are the larvae of the click beetle, and both have the annoying habit of biting through plant stems at soil level.

Fairly common in gardens and allotments, they prefer the softer stems of crops such as lettuce, and if tomatoes are planted out at a reasonably advanced stage the stems are usually thick enough to survive an attack. If young plants are found uprooted shortly after planting, the culprits are likely to be birds trying to get at the wireworms or cutworms attracted to the plants.

Tomato Leaf Miner

This is the larval stage of a fly which burrows inside the leaf and feeds on the soft tissue, causing characteristic serpentine 'mines'. The best way of dealing with this pest is to remove infected foliage and destroy it at a young stage to prevent the larva maturing (it exits the leaf, falls to the ground and pupates in the soil).

This pest can be around surprisingly early in the season, and for this reason closely inspect any bought-in plants for damage as it can be present at the propagation stage.

Damage caused by the tomato leaf miner – holes in the leaf by courtesy of the tomato moth.

Aphids

Familiar as greenfly but coming in a variety of colours, the problem with aphids is their potential to breed, and from just a few individuals the population can explode as soon as your back is turned. Like all insects, the length of the life cycle is dependent on temperature, and the warmer it is (up to a point), the quicker they can breed; thus aphid numbers will increase far more rapidly on plants in a greenhouse than on plants outside.

Aphids are sap feeders, and the plant is weakened by the sheer weight of numbers feeding. They also excrete much of the sugar they absorb from the sap, which covers the leaves in a glossy, sticky coating; this is unpleasant enough on its own, but it can itself be covered by an opportunist fungus called sooty mould. This does not attack the plant as such, it just grows on the sugary coating, but as it blocks out the light from the leaf surface it reduces the plant's photosynthetic ability. In really bad infestations sooty mould can get on the fruit (although this is not a disaster as it can be wiped off with a damp cloth and the fruit is unaffected).

Close inspection of the plants, concentrating on the lower leaf surfaces, is recommended to ascertain aphid numbers; also aphid infestations are rarely evenly distributed, so several plants can be relatively free, but one can be hit very badly. There are certain giveaways that can be seen from a casual glance:

- Glossy leaves (particularly lower leaves) caused by sugary secretions of aphids.
- White flecks on the leaf surfaces – as juvenile aphids grow and develop they shed their skins, and the white flecks are cast-off skins which remain scattered over the plant.
- Ants marching up the stem in their usual orderly fashion – ants farm aphids for their sugary secretions, and if ants are taking an interest in a plant then there are aphids about.

As regards control, what is chosen rather depends on how bad the infestation is, and on the individual grower's standpoint regarding the use of

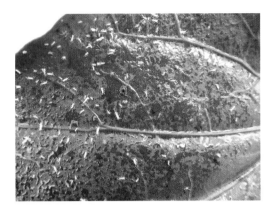

Leaves sticky with honeydew and covered in cast-off skins are a sure sign that aphids are about.

chemicals. There are compounds available at garden centres and similar outlets, which are supplied ready to use in a trigger gun. If these are used selectively so that only individual areas of heavy infestation are sprayed (individual plants, or maybe just the tops of plants), then the minimal amount of chemical is used, the operator is exposed to the chemical for the least amount of time, and it has the effect of thinning the population down rather than wiping it out – a tomato plant can tolerate a certain population of aphids to no ill effect, it is only when numbers get out of hand that damage is caused.

Alternatively the aphids can be controlled with a vacuum: this sounds like a joke, but has been done to apparent success. The recommendations from those who have developed the technique is to use a small, 12-volt hand-held car interior vacuum cleaner (powered from an old car battery), and to adapt it by taping a small paintbrush to the nozzle. The foliage is gently brushed, and the insects dislodged and sucked straight down the machine!

However, the principal method of controlling aphids is biological. Aphids and many other sap-feeding insects are attacked by a wide variety of other creatures, which for the purposes of biological control are classified into two categories:

- Predators – those that directly eat the pest.

- Parasites – those that use the pest as a nursery and food source for their young.

The Biological Control of Aphids

Introducing biological pest control into a crop has been practised for centuries in various parts of the world, and has developed into the main method of pest control used in the greenhouse production of long season crops such as tomato. Although techniques differ depending on the pest, the usual practice is to monitor the crop closely for the presence of pests, then while the population is still low, supplies of the appropriate biological control creatures are bought in from specialist raisers and released within the greenhouse. Following this, the whole pest/control balance is very carefully monitored, the objective being not to completely eradicate the pest, but to keep pest numbers down below the level at which they would cause economic damage. Further introductions of biological control are made as necessary.

Although it is possible for amateur growers with greenhouses to buy supplies of the same control creatures the commercial growers use, they rarely experience the same levels of success. A less demanding (and cheaper) approach is to encourage natural biological control into the area.

Ladybirds

Adult ladybird.

Ladybird larva.

Ladybird pupae.

and left in and around your tomatoes: as soon as the adult ladybirds hatch they will be hungry.

Hoverflies

Hoverflies resemble wasps, but usually start appearing a bit earlier than wasps. The larvae of the hoverfly feed on aphids, and adult hoverflies seek out large populations to deposit their eggs close by. Many flowering plants are attractive to hoverflies, and can be used to bring them into the area (*see* Companion Planting, page 105).

A source of ladybird pupae: these nettles held a high aphid population early in the season, providing plenty of food for ladybirds and resulting in a population explosion.

Both the adult and the larval forms of this beetle eat aphids, and soon show up where there are large populations. The problem is they usually find plants where the aphid population is greater than on your tomatoes. In years when the aphid population explodes, the ladybird population tends to follow because of the amount of food available. One way of encouraging ladybirds into the immediate area of your plants is to look for their pupal stage on plants that often have early summer aphid infestations (roses, flowering cherries and blackcurrants often get attacked early). A few of these pupae can be harvested on bits of leaf

Harvesting ladybird pupae – these should be placed in and around the tomato plants.

Hoverfly adult.

Hoverfly larva.

Lacewings

Attractive green insects with large wings, the larval stage of the lacewing feeds on aphids. Lacewings can be encouraged into the area by building them 'houses' in which to hibernate over the winter. This is not as strange as it first seems: hop growers in the UK were the first to provide lacewings with accommodation, and found that it worked very well, reducing their pesticide bills for very little effort.

Parasitic Wasps

Most damage is done to aphid populations by insects which are rarely, if ever, seen: tiny parasitic wasps. Inspect any leaf of a plant that has had aphids on it for a couple of weeks, and amongst the population you will see swollen, brown or bronze-coloured aphid bodies – these are usually called 'aphid mummies', and are what is left of the aphid once the wasp has done its work.

The wasp 'stings' the aphid to deposit a single egg into the body. Sometimes a cluster of aphid mummies is the work of a single wasp. The wasp's egg hatches, and its larva develops inside the aphid, eventually pupating inside the remains. Holding a group of aphid mummies up to the light will probably reveal that some have a small 'trap door' cut into the top of the abdomen: this is created when the adult wasp hatches from the pupa and cuts its way out.

Hoverfly pupa.

Aphid mummies, the result of parasitization by a tiny wasp.

Usually these wasps show up on their own, with no extra persuasion needed, though leaves from plants with aphid mummies can be collected, checked that they have not all hatched, then placed in and around tomatoes. For those growing other vegetables it is worth inspecting brassica leaves as they frequently yield a few aphid mummies.

A word of warning – when de-leafing tomatoes always turn the leaves over and check for the presence of unhatched aphid mummies; if there are any, leave the foliage around the base of the plants for a few days to give them time to hatch.

The Glasshouse Whitefly

The glasshouse whitefly is the most common pest of tomatoes in that it is guaranteed to show up every year – and unfortunately not confining its activities to greenhouse crops. A tiny white delta-winged insect resembling a minute moth, it is a sap feeder like the aphids and causes similar damage. Prior to the large-scale adoption of biological control methods in the early 1980s, commercial growers struggled to keep whitefly under control with chemical pesticides, as it

would quickly develop resistance; moreover, any new pesticide had only a limited lifespan before resistant strains of whitefly appeared.

Successful biological control of the whitefly has been achieved for many years by the use of a tiny, pinhead-sized parasitic wasp known as *Encarsia formosa*. These are supplied by post from specialist raisers and introduced into the glasshouse, where the real skill of the manager is to achieve a balance of the populations – which isn't easy, as the whitefly breeds about twice as fast as the wasp.

Perhaps as a result of milder winters and the continued use of *Encarsia formosa* (on a variety of greenhouse crops as well as tomato), *Encarsia* now seems to have gone native in the South of England, and will show up on outdoor plantings of tomato. The adult wasps are very seldom seen, but make their presence known by the parasitized whitefly 'scales' found on the underside of leaves. The scale acts as the pupal stage of the whitefly: unparasitized scales are green, but once the wasp has paid a visit, the scale turns black.

Interestingly, although non-native, *Encarsia formosa* was not deliberately introduced into the

Glasshouse whitefly, adult stage.

country, but somehow slipped in unnoticed, being first spotted attacking whitefly on a greenhouse tomato crop in the Lea Valley in the 1920s. The grower who owned the crop brought this to the attention of the local horticultural research station at Chesunt; entomologists there subsequently bred the wasps and handed them out to other growers in the area, and after a few years many growers were successfully using *Encarsia* for whitefly control. Were whitefly the only problem the practice might have continued, but other pests needed controlling as well as whitefly, and the chemicals available at the time also wiped out the *Encarsia*.

When the wonder pesticide DDT became available in the 1940s, it is perhaps not surprising that the growers went for this compound as the easy option that would kill everything, and commercial interest in the use of *Encarsia* faded away for the next forty years.

Red Spider Mite, or
Two-Spotted Spider Mite

Often mentioned in the same breath as whitefly as the other 'classic' pest of tomatoes, spider mite is a pest of warm conditions, often showing up on greenhouse or polytunnel crops, but less apparent on outdoor crops unless late summer conditions are particularly hot. The spider mites themselves are tiny and very difficult to see; the name is also confusing as the mites only turn brick red towards the autumn when the adults are preparing for hibernation – the rest of the time they are green. Because of their small size they are often not spotted until they are present in great numbers, and the feeding damage, which shows as a yellow speckling of the leaves, betrays their presence.

Heavy populations of mites congregate towards the tops of the plants, where a kind of webbing resembling fine cobwebs is produced. It is quite common to find only one plant in a population badly attacked in this way. Spider mites are another sap-feeding pest, and the sheer weight of numbers eventually overwhelms the plant.

Commercially, red spider mite is dealt with by introducing one or more types of predatory mite:

Encarsia formosa: whitefly parasite supplied as black parasitized whitefly 'scales' – these cards are hung up in the greenhouse for the wasps to hatch.

these are voracious feeders, and soon make short work of the pest. The best known of these is called *Phytoseiulus persimilis*, and of all the biological controls commercially available, this is the one that the amateur grower may have the best results with.

If greenhouse tomatoes are attacked by red spider mite late in the season (quite a common occurrence, particularly if early September conditions are warm) it is a worthwhile precaution pulling out the crop a bit earlier than usual, then taking the plants away from the greenhouse to hang them up and ripen the last of the fruit. This is because adult red spider mites can hibernate, seeking out cracks in the greenhouse structure, and lurk there until the following spring. By removing the plants early, hibernation can be prevented.

PLANT TONICS AND
NON-PESTICIDAL TREATMENTS

Often organic gardeners will say that if a plant is in a good state of health, then it is far more resistant to the attentions of pests and diseases than one that is growing under stressed conditions or is getting an unbalanced diet. This seems logical enough.

There are a number of preparations on the market which are applied as a spray or 'foliar feed' which have no toxic effects as such, so would not be classified as pesticides, but seem to act in a way that dissuades pests or makes the plant more resilient to pest or disease attack. Many of these are made from natural plant ingredients, particularly seaweeds, and tomatoes seem to have a particular affinity to seaweed. Growers in the Channel Islands and on the south coast of England have traditionally used seaweed as manure in tomato crops.

Compost Tea

Compost tea is used against a range of fungal diseases, and also seems to act as something of a plant tonic; its main use on tomatoes would appear to be in the seedling and young plant stages. A quite revolting but surprisingly successful concoction, it can be brewed up from kits of ingredients, or can be made from scratch. It is important that the brew is used fresh. Various recipes can be found, the common ingredients being:

- Very well rotted garden compost – some recipes specify manure-based compost.
- Water – rainwater is best; if using tap water, leave some buckets of it to stand for a few days to get rid of the chlorine.
- Some form of sugar – not included in all

Companion planting in a basket – tomato with *Tagetes* and basil.

recipes, but where it is, molasses seem to be favoured.

The ingredients are mixed together in a bucket or plastic dustbin, stirred well and left to ferment. The process is aided greatly by aeration, which can be provided by the type of small electrically powered air pump used in domestic aquaria. Fans of compost tea also say that the brewing should be done outdoors, as it is important to culture the bugs that survive at the ambient temperature. The resulting fermented liquid is alive with various micro-organisms, and is applied to the plants either as a spray, or more usually watered on to the roots.

The rule with compost tea seems to be to brew it regularly in small batches, and to use it very fresh. There has been some concern about using compost teas on plants with ripe fruit because of the small risk of E. coli bacteria from manure-based composts, so make sure any treatment with compost tea is done after picking.

Sodium and Potassium Bicarbonates

Both of these products are food-grade products; sodium bicarbonate or baking powder can be bought from the supermarket; potassium bicarbonate is not quite so readily available, being mainly used in food processing, so it may be more of a problem to locate some.

When mixed with water and used as a spray, both products have been shown to limit the spread of certain fungal diseases, particularly mildews.

Potassium bicarbonate may be preferable to the sodium form as most plants, particularly tomatoes, do not like too much sodium in their diet, whereas potassium is a major plant nutrient.

Companion Planting

This is a practice involving placing other plants in the close vicinity of the crop plant, with the idea of a mutually beneficial effect. One of the ideas behind companion planting is that the scent of the companion plant somehow masks the scent of the crop plant, so preventing certain pests finding it.

The best known companion plant for tomatoes is *Tagetes patula*, or French marigold. *Tagetes* is a very easy plant to grow, and the seed of the open-pollinated types is cheap enough, so this is well worth an experiment. *Tagetes* has scented foliage and flowers, and the scent is most apparent in the full sun; it is also very attractive to hoverflies. There is also evidence that root exudates from *tagetes* are toxic to soil-living nematodes, which could be useful on soil-grown crops. At the end of the season the *tagetes* plants should be dug into the soil to get the full benefit.

Tagetes minuta: This seems a ridiculous name for a plant that grows to 6ft (2m) tall, but the specific name actually refers to the tiny flowers it produces. This is not one to use for companion planting due to its extreme size, but if grown elsewhere in the garden a few of its highly aromatic leaves can be harvested regularly (some people report skin irritation from handling the foliage, so wear gloves) and scattered around the plants.

(*See also* Chapter 10 for raising companion plants.)

Garlic: Of less interest as a companion plant as it is usually autumn planted and harvested in the summer, garlic can be used to mask the scent of the plant, or in many cases persuade insects already feeding on the plant to leave. It is also said to have fungicidal properties due to its high content of sulphur compounds.

The American preparation 'garlic barrier' has been around for about ten years and has been used in many aspects of horticulture for pest control. In addition to this, other garlic-based products are now becoming more widely available. Garlic tea involves brewing up some crushed or sliced garlic cloves in hot water to make an extract. Rather than being sprayed on to the plants it should be watered on to the roots; the plant then absorbs it into the vascular system leaving the whole plant garlic flavoured, which is offputting to sap-feeding pests. Providing this is not done to excess, the fruit does not get tainted.

10 TOMATO MISCELLANY

SAVING YOUR OWN SEED

Many gardeners would not consider saving seed from a tomato crop, but to do so is a fairly simple process if a little messy, and as a tomato can contain up to 200 seeds there is no danger of having to sacrifice any significant number of edible fruits. One important thing to remember: do not save seed from F1 hybrid varieties, as the offspring of these will not come true to type.

Usually the two main reasons for saving seed are to maintain a particular variety, usually a heritage or heirloom type, the seed of which is no longer commercially available; or to propagate a single plant or a small number of plants that have shown some particular valuable characteristic, either by accident or design (for example, perhaps being less affected by disease than others).

Seed Saving to Maintain a Variety

In the commercial world, to maintain a variety plant breeders and seed growers look for 'trueness to type' in the seed crop – in other words, they know what the variety should look like, and in growing plants for a seed crop they employ a process of inspection and 'rogueing', often starting at the seedling stage, in which all plants that are widely different (known as 'off types' or 'rogues') are gradually removed from the stock, so that the final collection of plants which are to produce the seed crop do not contain any elements which are not typical of that variety.

With tomatoes being mainly self-pollinated, individual varieties tend to remain reasonably stable and true to type from one generation to the next. With any non-hybrid (open-pollinated)

OPPOSITE: A lush crop of tomato fruit is the reward for choosing the right growing conditions.

RIGHT: A tomato miscellany.

plants there is always a little variability, which is recognized as being valuable, so in looking for 'off types' in a tomato crop you are only looking for plants which are obviously different from the herd, not just a tiny bit different.

The approach to seed saving should be to collect fruit from a number of plants that are representative of the variety; this is to preserve the natural variability. If fruit is only taken from one or two individuals this is essentially selecting within the variety, and some of the variability could be lost.

As a general rule, take one or two fruits from each plant that is true to type, mix together and extract the seeds as a bulk. For individual gardeners this will obviously give more seed than can realistically be used, but there are plenty of 'seed savers' networks, so it will not be difficult to find the surplus a good home.

Seed Saving from Selected Plants

If you spot an individual plant amongst your crop that appears to display some characteristic that could be valuable, it is worth putting a label on it to remind you to save some seed, grow the saved seed next year and see if this characteristic is passed on to the next generation. Although tomatoes are largely self-pollinating, plant breeders would grow such plants in isolation – that is to say, removed from the close proximity of other tomatoes, which would lessen any chance of cross pollination taking place – however, in the garden this is difficult to achieve.

Selecting the Fruit

Fruit selected for seed production should be taken from disease-free plants and be 100 per cent ripe. Cracked fruit (particularly late season) is not necessarily a problem so long as *Botrytis* has not started to invade. It is sometimes recommended to harvest the fruit and keep it indoors for a few days to make sure it is fully ripe before extracting the seed.

In his *Commercial Greenhouse Crops* of 1950

Scooping out the pulp to extract the seeds.

Walter Bewley recommends that fruit from the first truss is not taken for seed extraction, as the seed appears to have impaired germination. He goes on to suggest that fruit from the second and third trusses seems to be the best for the job.

It is tempting to leave any seed-saving activities to the end of the growing season and use the last of the fruit; this can be risky, however, and any seed saving should be accompanied by a germination test, and if the germination proves to be poor, perhaps due to insufficient pollination late in the season, then the seed may hardly be worth keeping and the opportunity has been lost if no more fruit are available.

Fermenting tomato pulp; the process has nearly come to an end, and the viable seeds are dropping to the bottom of the jar.

Extracting the Seed

The seeds are suspended in a type of gel that contains germination inhibitors. The process of extraction involves removing the seeds and gel from the fruit, breaking down the gel by fermentation or by using a chemical, then making sure all traces of the gel are washed off the seeds before they are carefully dried.

A glass or glazed ceramic container should be used, as these are unaffected by the acids in the tomato. Cut the fruit in half transversely, and scoop out the gel and seeds with a spoon.

Fermentation Method

For small quantities just scoop the gel into a jam jar; if it is particularly thick, add a little water, then put the lid on the jar, give it a good shake and put it somewhere warm – 18 to 20°C is about right, but be careful of higher temperatures, because if it is too warm the seed could start to germinate.

Check on the jar daily, or twice daily if at all possible, and give it a shake or stir on each occasion – you may be able to observe bubbles as the mixture ferments, and as it proceeds you should see the seeds beginning to separate out and fall to the bottom. After about three days the process should be complete, and the seeds need removing without delay as they will now have lost their germination inhibitor and could start into growth.

To help the next stage it is often worth adding a little more water to the jar to approximately double the original volume, then leaving it for an hour or so as this helps everything settle out into two layers: pulp and light, non-viable seed floats to the top, and heavy, viable seeds remain in a layer at the bottom.

Most of the remaining pulp floating on top can then be scooped off with a spoon before tipping the seeds and other liquid into a kitchen sieve and washing thoroughly under running water. Rubbing the seeds with the back of a wooden spoon while washing helps loosen any material still sticking to the seed coats.

Soda Method

To speed up the seed extraction process for the busy nurseryman, the following method was developed in the 1920s, a time when many growers saved their own seed. Scoop out the seeds and pulp as before, and place in a glass container, then approximately double the volume by topping it up with a solution of 5 per cent washing soda (made by dissolving 50g soda crystals in one litre of water or pro rata), stir well and leave somewhere warm – 18 to 20°C; the seeds should then drop out of the mix in about twelve hours. Rinse and dry as before.

This process darkens the seed coats, but no harm is done.

Drying

It is important to dry the seeds quickly – tip them on to kitchen towel to remove most of the water, then spread them out on to the surface of a mirror (or a sheet of glass) to dry thoroughly (they can be dried fully on paper towel but they tend to stick to it). Drying should be done at room temperature and out of direct sunlight, as temperatures in excess of 32°C can cause damage.

Once dry to the touch, the seeds need a further two to four weeks for the internal moisture content to stabilize before they can be packed and stored. Place the seeds in a paper envelope and leave it somewhere dry where the temperature is cool and relatively constant.

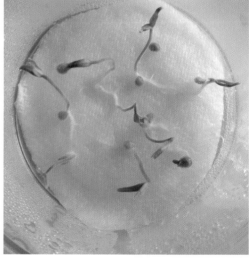

Germination Test

Before storing the seed away for the following season, it is advisable to do a germination test just to make sure the seed is all right and is worth keeping. Take a small sample, maybe ten seeds, put them in a shallow dish inside a folded paper towel, wet the towel thoroughly and leave in a temperature of 18–21°C for four to five days. Check the seeds from about day four: if healthy roots are starting to emerge, then all is well. Don't be too concerned if not all the seeds germinate – seven out of ten is reasonable.

If some mould starts to appear on the seed coats and paper it may just be some opportunist fungi such as a bread mould, which probably means the seeds collected some spores whilst drying. This is not usually a problem and should not affect germination.

Packing and Storing

It is difficult to replicate the hermetically sealed packets used by commercial seedsmen, but the object of the exercise is to keep the seeds' moisture content constant once it has stabilized after extraction. Most regular seed savers become good at improvising: popular solutions are small 'zip-lock' self-sealing plastic bags, which give plenty of room for a label, or plastic 35mm film containers which suit larger quantities, don't easily get lost, and allow easy sowing of the seed direct from the container.

If storage temperatures are kept fairly low and as constant as possible the seed will remain viable for two to three years, occasionally longer.

TOMATO PLANTS FROM CUTTINGS

As tomatoes will easily produce adventitious roots from the stem with the slightest amount of persuasion, it is very easy to propagate tomato plants from cuttings, but the practice is not commonplace. Sideshoots removed from indeterminate plants as a routine operation can easily be rooted – simply re-cut the stem at right angles to give a clean cut (there is no need to cut to a node as with many types of cutting, as the tomato will push out adventitious roots all along the stem). Remove much of the foliage – large leaves can be cut in half rather than removed totally – insert into a pot of seed or rooting compost, and water thoroughly.

ABOVE: **Trimming a sideshoot to make a cutting.**

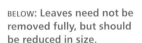

BELOW: **Leaves need not be removed fully, but should be reduced in size.**

Windowsill propagation of cuttings; a green bottle is used to give partial shade.

The cuttings then need to be enclosed to give conditions of high humidity – a plastic bag over the top is often used, or the top two-thirds of a 2ltr (3.5-pint) plastic bottle.

Place the cuttings and cover on a sunny windowsill; if it is particularly sunny, use a brown or green plastic bottle rather than a clear one, as this will prevent leaf scorch.

Leave undisturbed for five days – balance the top on the bottle rather than screw it on, and remove it totally once in a while to allow the condensation to clear.

Remove the cover on day five, water the pot, check the cuttings, remove anything that has died, and trim off any foliage that has started to die back. The cuttings will usually be well on their way to rooting by now, but replace the cover for another three to four days to make sure that the roots are well developed before the new plant is potted up.

Once potted, give the new plant three to four days in a shaded environment to acclimatize before exposing to full sun – the usual response of the plant to stress at this stage is to stop growing, and possibly abort any developing flowers.

A rooted tomato cutting from a sideshoot.

GRAFTING TOMATO PLANTS

A grafted plant consists of two parts: the rootstock, and the above-ground part that is called the scion. The technique of joining the two together is known as grafting, and it is a practice associated more with fruit trees and vines than annual crops.

As species within a genus are usually compatible to be grafted together, so the tomato can be successfully grafted on to a potato giving a plant yielding both crops – this may seem ideal for those short of space, but in reality the plant doesn't yield much of either, but is just an interesting curiosity. Commercially, tomato and aubergine (eggplant) are sometimes grafted together: in Europe the tomato is used as a rootstock for eggplant, which puts more vigour into the eggplant giving higher yields; in Taiwan the opposite combination is used – eggplant is used as a rootstock for tomato, as eggplant roots are

tolerant to waterlogged soils during the wet season. Usually, though, tomato is grafted on to another tomato – a specially bred rootstock type.

Grafting may be done for a number of reasons, but the main ones for tomato are to put more vigour into the scion giving higher yields, or to use a rootstock which is resistant or tolerant to root diseases and damage by nematode (eelworm). The first commercial tomato rootstocks became available in 1958, and grafting practice developed through the 1960s. The rootstock used for many years was known as KNVF, which was an acronym of its resistance capabilities, standing for corky root, nematode, *verticillium* and *fusarium*; later it changed to PNVF, using the Latin generic name of corky root disorder *pyrenochaeta*.

Grafted plants became quite popular for commercial growers as greenhouse tomato production became more intensive and tomatoes were grown on the same sites year after year.

Having plants resistant to soil-borne diseases was a possible alternative to soil sterilization by steam, which was an expensive option. With the advent of F1 hybrid tomatoes with increased levels of disease resistance, and the increased popularity of soil-less cropping in the UK and Europe from the mid-1970s onwards, the practice declined in commercial usage, though organic growers, who have to grow their plants in the soil to comply with the rules for organic status, recognized its advantages and persevered with it.

Interestingly we have now come full circle, and a new generation of rootstocks is on the market, and mainstream commercial tomato production is back using grafted plants for vigour and disease resistance.

Why Try Grafted Plants?

If tomatoes are grown on the same site year after year, they are a good precaution against a range of soil-borne diseases. Grafted plants also display more vigour than plants on their own roots, and recover more quickly from periods of stress (such as a sudden hot spell). The best sources of grafted tomato plants are specialist plant raisers. Those wishing to try grafting for themselves may have to shop around quite widely to source seeds of tomato rootstocks in sufficiently small quantities; the old KNVF (or PNVF) which was once widely available now seems to be no more, and few seed suppliers appear to list the modern types.

It has been suggested that grafting 'heirloom' types using a modern F1 hybrid as the rootstock is worthwhile, as the vigour of the F1 pushes the older variety into more rapid growth and earlier fruiting, also conferring any disease resistance in the F1 hybrid to the scion variety. Though unproven, there could well be some value in this; recent research comparing modern cultivars with those introduced in the 1950s indicated that modern cultivars have higher photosynthetic rates and generally grow more quickly.

Grafting Procedure

The method of grafting used commercially is usually called the Japanese method, and involves grafting the plants in the seedling stage when the stems are only about 1.5mm in diameter. The

Seeds of 'Beaufort' and 'Maxifort' rootstocks.

ABOVE: 'Topping' the rootstock at a 45-degree angle.

RIGHT: Rootstock with grafting clip attached.

stems are carefully cut through at 45 degrees, and the top of the scion variety is joined to the rootstock using a special plastic clip, which also incorporates provision for a support stick to keep the whole thing upright while the graft unites.

This method is not entirely practical for the amateur grower, as the plants need very controlled conditions of temperature and humidity for the grafts to unite; also the type of grafting clip used is difficult to obtain in small numbers. Less fiddly and easier for the amateur to do is the approach graft, which involves raising both the rootstock and scion varieties to a larger size, then a flap of tissue is raised on both plants by cutting into each stem for about a third of its thickness. The plants are then joined together by interlocking these and holding them together with a couple of inches of ordinary household sticky tape. Both plants are then potted together, and the top taken out of the rootstock to prevent further extension growth.

When the graft unites after about ten days a plant is formed with one growing point and two root systems; however, it is usual to leave the root on the scion variety at this stage, as the plant suffers a check to growth if it is removed. If using a commercial rootstock the root on the scion cultivar can be left in place, as the rootstock is so vigorous it soon takes over. If using any other combination (say, a heritage type on to an F1 rootstock), wait until the final planting stage before snipping off the scion root, to give the graft plenty of time to unite and grow strong.

When planting grafted plants, it is important to keep the graft union above the level of the soil or compost.

GROWING TOMATOES ORGANICALLY

It is important to differentiate between what a gardener would classify as organic production, and what is defined as organic production for commercial purposes. Commercial growers producing crops to certified organic standards have to work to very strict guidelines regarding all aspects of crop production, from using organic seed and plant-raising compost to using only fertilizers that are approved for organic production and relying on biological methods of pest and disease control. Also as the regulations currently stand, the crop has to be soil grown.

To many people who grow their own produce, organic production would essentially mean the avoidance of chemical pesticides and artificial fertilizers. A visit to a garden centre can lead to some confusion, as a number of products bear the name 'organic' or in some way align themselves as being compatible with organic production methods. The following is a short summary on the main differences between these and similar but 'conventional' products.

Scion inserted into a grafting clip.

Approach grafting – cut down into the rootstock…

…and up into the scion.

Bring the two plants together and engage the cut sections...

...and join with tape.

Keep the graft union above the level of the compost when potting.

Organic seed: The seed crop was grown according to certified organic standards using only the allowable inputs, and following harvest the seed has not been chemically treated in any way. Seed from European companies may bear the title 'biological' or 'ecological' instead of 'organic'.

Organic compost: Contains only approved fertilizers, and the bulk ingredients come from sustainable or renewable sources. Favoured bulk ingredients are coir (coconut fibre) and composted bark.

Organic fertilizers: From plant, animal or occasionally mineral sources, the common factor is that to release the plant nutrients the material has to be further broken down by the activity of soil organisms. Usually these fertilizers release their nutrients slowly, which makes them useful for long-season crops such as tomatoes, and safer for the heavy-handed.

Organically approved pesticides: These are fairly few and far between, as one of the main tenets of organic growing is preventing the problem. Most products that are intended to kill sap-feeding insects such as aphids and whitefly are based on non-toxic materials such as soft soap or vegetable oils (which kills by clogging up the insects' breathing mechanism), or alternatively on natural pyrethrum (extracted from *Chrysanthemum cinerarifolium*) which is toxic to insects.

With commercial production of tomatoes the days of heavy pesticide inputs are thankfully long gone, most of the pest control being achieved by biological means; however, the need to return to cropping in the soil has placed limitations on how far growers are willing to go with organic production.

Propagating Companion Plants

Companion plants and herbs are usually grown from seed starting in about late April, which should be convenient as they can use propagation space vacated when tomatoes are planted out.

Marigolds

Marigolds are the best known companion plant for tomatoes, particularly the French marigold *Tagetes patula*. These have large, elongated seeds with a tuft on one end (the remains of part of the flower), which makes them easy to pick up and sow individually.

The easiest way of propagating marigolds for companion planting work is to sow the seeds directly into a small pot – eight to ten seeds in a 9cm (3.5in) pot is about right, and let them grow as a clump. This saves a job by avoiding the pricking out stage. Plant the entire potful when the first flowers are starting to show.

If the dead flowers are removed once in a while (deadheading) they will continue to flower all summer.

Nasturtium (Tropaeolum)

The scent of the flowers is considered to be off-putting to certain pests, but nasturtium often works as a trap plant for aphids, which are more attracted to it than to tomatoes. The large-leaved *Tropaeolum vulgare* should be planted in a large pot with several support canes as it is very vigorous, or grown in a hanging basket and allowed to trail. The smaller cultivar forms of *Tropaeolum majus nanum* can be included around the plants. Young nasturtium leaves can be eaten in salads.

A very easy plant to grow, nasturtiums have large seeds which are best sown individually into pots; to speed germination some growers soak the seed in a saucer of water for twelve hours before sowing.

Alliums

Garlic is well known as a companion plant with the ability to discourage flying insects, but most garlic is planted in the autumn and is well on its way to harvest by the time it would be useful around tomatoes. It is possible to obtain late garlic plants by planting some cloves of culinary garlic around the tomatoes, but these tend to die off quite quickly from midsummer as day length reduces.

The common chives, the purple-flowered

Regular fruit shape and size are the result of good pollination and seed development.

Allium schoenoprasum and the slower growing white-flowered Chinese or garlic chives *Allium tuberosum* are both worth growing, particularly to accompany plants in containers or hanging baskets. The easiest way to use them is to buy a well established pot and divide up the clump. At the end of the season re-pot them, or plant out in the garden.

Basil

Ocimum basilicum is the classic herb to accompany tomatoes, and also one of the easiest to grow. It is sometimes mentioned as a useful companion plant, but a great deal of basil is needed for the scent to have any effect in warding off insects. If allowed to grow to maturity the flowers are attractive to pollinating insects and hoverflies.

There are several different types of basil, the most familiar being the large-leaved or Genovese type as often sold in supermarkets. This is the quickest growing type, but tends to get a bit straggly and untidy looking unless regularly picked over. The small-leaved type, usually just referred to as 'bush', is preferred for tomatoes in pots or hanging baskets as it forms smaller clumps and doesn't take over. The purple-leaved and ruffled types can also be used to add interest to a hanging basket or pot, and for further variety try the lemon-scented *Ocimum citriodorum*.

All basils are easy to grow from seed, though the purple types are very much slower to grow than the green types. They can be direct seeded into small pots providing the sowing is done thinly, as they all seem prone to damping off disorders at a young stage.

Basil freezes very well with no preparation; just pack short lengths of cut stem into a plastic bag and freeze, and it can be used as required.

Oregano

For pizza and pasta dishes, oregano is easy, if a bit slow to grow from seed, so many prefer to buy a ready-established plant. It is best grown in a separate pot rather than planted amongst the tomatoes, as in its natural environment it grows on fairly impoverished soils. It likes good drainage, so add some grit to the usual potting compost and keep the plants fairly dry.

Coriander

Leaf coriander or cilantro is another easy subject; use a tall pot as the plant has a long taproot, and just space sow the large seeds. Grow several pots so the leaves can be cut as needed and the plant given time to recover. Successional sowings may be needed to keep up the supply through the season as the plant quickly flowers and runs to seed in midsummer.

FURTHER INFORMATION

SEED SUPPLIERS

Kings Seeds
Monks Farm
Kelvedon
Colchester
Essex
CO5 9PG
http://www.kingsseeds.com/

Marshalls Seeds (also young plants)
S E Marshall & Co
Alconbury Hill
Huntingdon
Cambs
PE28 4HY
http://www.marshalls-seeds.co.uk

Nicky's Nursery Ltd.
Fairfield Road
Broadstairs
Kent CT10 2JU
http://www.nickys-nursery.co.uk

Real Seeds
PO Box 18
Newport
Fishguard
Pembrokeshire
SA65 0AA
http://www.realseeds.co.uk/

Simpsons Seeds (also young plants)
The Walled Garden Nursery
Horningsham
Warminster
BA12 7NQ
http://www.simpsonsseeds.co.uk/

Suttons Seeds (also young plants)
Suttons Consumer Products Limited
Woodview Road
Paignton, Devon
TQ4 7NG
http://www.suttons.co.uk

Thompson & Morgan
Poplar Lane
Ipswich
IP8 3BU
http://www.thompson-morgan.com/

Edwin Tucker & Sons Ltd
Brewery Meadow
Stonepark
Ashburton
Newton Abbot
Devon TQ13 7DG
http://www.tuckers-seeds.co.uk/

SUPPLIERS OF YOUNG PLANTS

Organic Plants
Benwick Road
Doddington
March
Cambridgeshire
PE15 0TU
http://www.organicplants.co.uk/

Vegetable Plants Direct
Sparra Park Cottage
Upper Tamar Lake
Bude
Cornwall
EX23 9SB
http://www.vegetableplantsdirect.co.uk

SUPPLIERS OF BIOLOGICAL PEST CONTROL, FLEECE COVERS AND SUNDRIES

Agralan Ltd
The Old Brickyard
Ashton Keynes
Swindon
Wiltshire
SN6 6QR
www.Agralan.co.uk

Defenders Ltd.
Occupation Road
Wye
Ashford
Kent
TN25 5EN
www.defenders.co.uk

Green Gardener
Chandlers End
Mill Road
Stokesby
Great Yarmouth
NR29 3EY
www.greengardener.co.uk

Just Green
Unit 14
Springfield Road Industrial Estate
Burnham-on-Crouch
Essex CM0 8UA
www.Just-green.com

GENERAL

The British Tomato Growers Association represents commercial tomato growers in the UK; their website www.britishtomatoes.co.uk has all sorts of interesting tomato-related material.

Garden Organic www.gardenorganic.org.uk is the working name of the Henry Doubleday Research Association (HDRA). Their heritage seed library collects and maintains stocks of heritage and heirloom varieties; joining the library gives members access to a range of these, seed stocks permitting.

To review all plants being trialled by the **Royal Horticultural Society** and further information about the Award of Garden Merit (AGM) see the 'plant trials and awards' section of the RHS website http://www.rhs.org.uk/Plants/Plant-trials-and-awards.

INDEX

OTHER GARDENING BOOKS FROM CROWOOD

Blackburne-Maze, Peter *The Complete Guide to Fruit Growing*
Blackburne-Maze, Peter *The Complete Guide to Vegetable Growing*
Cox, Freda *Garden Styles*
Cunningham, Sally, *Ecological Gardening*
Gray, Linda, *Herb Gardening*
Gregson, Sally, *Ornamental Vegetable Gardening*
Gregson, Sally, *Practical Propagation*
Hodge, Geoff, *Pruning*
Jones, Peter, *Gardening on Clay*
Littlewood, Michael, *The Organic Gardener's Handbook*
Marder, John, *Water-Efficient Gardening*
Nottridge, Rhoda, *Wildlife Gardening*
Saunders, Bridgette, *Allotment Gardening*